Desirable Men

How to Find Them

Dr. Romance

PRIMA PUBLISHING

PRIMA PUBLISHING and colophon are registered trademarks of Prima Communications, Inc.

Library of Congress Cataloging-in-Publication Data

Fagan, Nancy.
    Desirable men: how to find them / Nancy Fagan.
        p.   cm.
    Includes index.
    ISBN 0-7615-0625-X
    1. Mate selection.   2. Man-woman relationships.   I. Title.
    HQ801.F24   1996
    646.7'7—dc20   96-31338
                                                                    CIP

96 97 98 99 00 01 HH 10 9 8 7 6 5 4 3 2 1
Printed in the United States of America

How to Order:
Single copies may be ordered from Prima Publishing, P.O. Box 1260BK, Rocklin, CA 95677; telephone (916) 632-4400. Quantity discounts are also available. On your letterhead, include information concerning the intended use of the books and the number of books you wish to purchase.

Visit us online at http://www.primapublishing.com

To my son Brandon
who is and will always be
number one in my life.
I love you "baby."

This book is also dedicated
to my future husband
who will be caught as
a result of my using the
techniques in this book.

Contents

Dear Diary . . .

May 6, 1963.
Hospital Delivery Room.

"Look Eric," Mother says, "There's a little red heart on Nancy's bottom. Cupid must have branded her." Dad smiles amused and says, "This should be interesting!"

1

Your Coming-Out Party

As you'll note from the diary notation at the opening of this book, that's the way it all started. And Dad was right. It's been either one thing or another in the arena of love and romance ever since. I will share more of my real-life diary with you, but you will have to wait until the next chapter. So stay tuned because you will laugh as you identify with my adventures . . . and failures.

In the meantime, congratulations. By obtaining this special book, you've taken an important step toward finding a desirable man. One who will love you, cherish you, and treat you the way you should be treated. Trust me on this one. Many women have followed this simple formula, and it works beautifully. They have found partners who treat them well, and the same will occur for you.

How often does this happen to you? It's late Friday afternoon, and you are exhausted after a long week. You're driving home, craving the minute you can finally have some peace and quiet. One hour later, your exhaustion turns to loneliness. You feel isolated, bored, and sad. All you can think about is getting back to work on Monday morning to get your mind off being alone.

Well, according to the 1990 U.S. census report, many women are in the same boat: 47.5 percent of women in the United States are single. This figure can be broken down into 24 percent of women who have never been married, 12 percent who are widowed, 9.5 percent who are divorced, and 2.5 percent who are separated. That makes for a lot of single women.

Many women take offense when they are minimized to a statistical number directed toward the sensitive area of being single. But, as you know, being single means much more than being a number—it has personal meaning and emotions for everyone who is in the situation. Each woman who is single is so for unique reasons, none of which are bad; they are just the result of choices and circumstances. Many women who will read this book fall into one of the census's statistical groups. If they don't, then they are probably traveling in that direction. Let's now take a look at each group and see some examples of why the women are there.

The first category of single women—the 24 percent who "have never been married" group—are there for many reasons:

- They took the time to find themselves and now find themselves with no one else.
- They got pregnant early and never married.
- They focused on their education or career.
- They got involved with "Mr. Right-Now," which lasted many years but never led to a marriage proposal.
- Their engagement was called off.
- They found the "right" one just to watch him turn into "Mr. Wrong."
- Their boyfriend was married and never left his wife.
- Their fiancé died.
- Their fiancé married someone else.
- They have a disability and hide from the world.
- They have sexual identity issues or confusion.

The second category of single women is the 12 percent who are widows, with a large percentage being in a higher age bracket.

- They are still in love with the departed husband.
- They are older women who have a small pool of available men to choose from. The few men who are single appear to have a line of women three blocks long who bear gifts in his pursuit.

- They are women whose loss was so great that they are unable to love and lose another.

The third category of single women is the 9.5 percent in the "divorced" category, who are there for these reasons:

- They can't explain why the marriage ended.
- They grew apart from their ex-husband.
- They had an affair and fell in love with the man.
- The husband had an affair that ended the marriage.
- The man had a problem with drugs, alcohol, or gambling.
- The husband was abusive.
- The husband was emotionally unavailable.
- They no longer loved the husband.
- The husband changed too much to be acceptable.
- They decided it would be better to be alone than to continue with that mate.
- They waited for the children to leave the house.
- There were too many strains in the marriage.
- They tried marital counseling, and it didn't help.

The final category of single women—the 2.5 percent who are in the "separated" group—are in that situation for the following reasons:

- Their husbands have cheated on them.
- Their husbands have asked them for a divorce.
- They are working on their marriage.
- Their husband is in jail.
- They have left their husbands.
- They are trying to find themselves.
- They chose their career over their marriage.

Sometimes a stigma is attached to being single, so people make excuses for why they are. You have no need to be ashamed for being in the situation you are in. If being single wasn't a choice you made, it is nothing to be embarrassed about. Keep in mind that 47 percent of the single population are women who feel the way you do—alone. Most would prefer to be in a good relationship than to be without one. If you disagree with this point, it is more than likely because the men in your past relationships did not fulfill your basic needs. On the other hand, if you have experienced satisfaction in a relationship, then you know there is nothing like having a companion who loves you. Life is meant to be shared, to have a man to support you when you risk, to hold you when you fail, and to love you just because he treasures you.

Many times being alone is what drives a woman to get involved with the wrong men for temporary comfort, but nothing more. Don't make that mistake this time around and let the wrong reasons dictate your happiness by compromising your choice in a mate. If desire for love is at the core of every waking moment, it's time to make some changes in your life and find the partner who's right for you.

The main ingredient you need for finding a partner is *desire*. By purchasing this book, you've shown that you have that special measure of desire to change things. Perhaps you've tried for a long time to find that special person with the glass slipper that fits only your foot. Fairy tales do come true, and I'm here to help you find your prince.

This will be an exciting journey, one that will positively affect the rest of your life. Don't become too serious about this search, though. A good sense of humor is important in life, especially on the journey to finding your ideal man.

Let's get started. I'm anxious to guide you through a fun and exciting process. Turn the page because he's waiting.

P.S. A note for the male readers: If you recognize yourself in this book, you may be right and you may be wrong. But you'll never know for sure because the names have been changed to protect the innocent (or not so innocent).

———————

Dear Diary . . .

Dressed in a vibrant red dress. Conservative, but sexy. He's sure to salivate. Optimistic. I sit, waiting for Lou from the personals ad to arrive. His ad read, "to die for." And that was about to happen.

Entering the building, he excitedly walks up. In a wind-storm of bad breath, he introduces himself, displaying a broad mouth full of jagged yellow teeth. Oh, my! No thanks. Undesirable man. I immediately want to move to Death Valley to find better sights and smells. Conclusion: He's not Mr. Right.

2

Roadblocks

In the search for a relationship, women find many reasons that they are not involved with a man. These excuses are referred to as *roadblocks* in this book. They are the rationalizations that prevent women from having the relationships they would like to have. Look at the list here to get an idea of typical roadblocks women encounter. Place a check next to any item that applies to you. When you complete the list, fill in other reasons that you have had a difficult time finding the relationship you want.

- ☐ I don't have time to look for a relationship.
- ☐ All the good men are taken.
- ☐ I'm tired of looking for a partner.
- ☐ I'm too shy to meet men.
- ☐ Men have too much baggage.
- ☐ I am still getting over my last relationship.
- ☐ I don't want to settle for the kind of men out there.
- ☐ I have a better chance of being abducted by aliens.
- ☐ I'm afraid of rejection.
- ☐ I can never find a baby-sitter, and when I do it's too expensive.
- ☐ I can't find someone who shares my interests.

☐ I don't feel good about myself.

☐ I don't want to give up my freedom.

Please list your roadblocks:

_____

_____

_____

_____

_____

Reasons for Roadblocks

I've found that women tell themselves, over and over, unrealistic reasons that they have not found a relationship. These excuses become self-fulfilling prophecies, acting as the script they follow. Generally, the negative and helpless expectation they profess will come to fruition. The end result is that they are alone because of that very excuse they blamed it on.

I've given seminars many times on how to find a desirable man. I start off the seminar with two questions: "Has anyone here had problems meeting quality single men, or just meeting singles, period?" and "What are a few of those problems?" As we go around the room, the women chuckle when they hear the blatant rationalizations some women use to explain why they are single. As I hear the roadblocks, I write them on the board for all to witness. When everyone is finished giving their excuses, an interesting pattern emerges. All of the "unique" reasons for being alone fall into one of several categories. These categories are listed at the beginning of this chapter. In the seminar, the women come up with new ways to overcome each issue. In this book, I will go over the issues in the upcoming chapters. But for now, let me remind you that it is not comfortable to take the blame for being alone. It is so much easier to have an excuse to blame it on. The truth is hard to take, but the only reason women are single is because of their lack of a proactive approach to resolve the situation.

Please, Tell Me Another One . . .

I have heard all kinds of excuses, but none more heartfelt than the one from a San Diego seminar. Looking to the back of the room, a young woman in a wheelchair raised her hand to share her roadblock with the class. As I gestured for her to talk, all the women, one by one, became quiet as they listened to her former roadblock. She stated the obviousness of her condition and explained how she locked herself away for eight years after her accident. She truly believed that no one could love her the way she was. For eight years she was alone, longing for a man to share her life with. One day, she explained, she picked up her phone book looking for a support group to commiserate with. Instead, she came across a singles club for people with disabilities. It took her three months to build up the nerve to go. However, once there, she realized that she had wasted eight years of her life blaming her physical disability for her lack of a relationship. Her situation was atypical and touching, but she overcame it.

Okay, you may not be physically disabled, but you still have excuses. Take Carol. Her roadblock is much more common. She complains that men use her for sex and then leave her. First, Carol has a background of abuse. As a little girl, she was sexually molested by her father. For years he told her that all she was good for was sexually relieving him. And since her mother wouldn't have sex with him, it was her job. She loved her father but hated what he did to her. It was the only time he paid attention to her, so she figured it was better than nothing. The abuse finally ended when she was 11, but the damage stayed with her.

When I first met Carol, she was dressed provocatively. In conversation she made many sexual innuendos. She learned to get a man's attention through her sexy appearance and sexual offerings. Carol gave off the message that all she was good for was sex, so that's what the men took from her. Well, since Carol has a history of abusive relationships with men, she feels comfortable in this role. She doesn't like the abuse, but it is all she knows. Carol, like many women who have been abused, have low self-esteem and settle for much less than they deserve. Carol got into therapy for incest survivors and built her self-worth up. She learned to attract men who wanted to get to know her, not just her body. Carol was married earlier this year and couldn't be happier.

Another example is that of Betty, an attractive 42-year-old. She believed she was doing everything right until she came to me for private consultations. She kept herself in shape, dressed nicely, and was socially active. As a matter of fact, her business was arranging singles dances. Our first meeting consisted of finding a compatible type of man for her to focus her search on. She matched up nicely with businessmen, so our second meeting was at a coffee shop where many of these men went. She seemed relaxed until we got in line to buy our coffee. Instantly her body language changed. She looked uncomfortable. She clung to her purse, stood stiff, and tapped her foot nervously. She certainly got her fair share of admiring glances but was too locked in her nervousness to even notice. When we sat down at a table, she relaxed a little until she became aware of an attractive man looking at her. I commented on her body language, explaining my interpretation of her body positioning. She explained to me that she was afraid of rejection. So for Betty, it was easier rejecting men before they could reject her.

During our next consultation, we practiced ways to deal with nervousness and improving body language. She needed to learn how to send inviting messages to men. Betty has improved greatly and now dates regularly. She learned that her nervousness around men caused her body language to appear uninterested to the admirers.

Sometimes, as in the case of the woman in the wheelchair, finding a social group that attracts others like yourself is a good place to start your search. This can be a singles group for people of a certain nationality, a religiously oriented group, or even a group for retired people. For women like Carol, insight into your past is a good start. By understanding the past, it allows you to prevent the same patterns in your future. For women like Betty, all you need to do is make slight changes in your body language to let men know it is okay to approach you. Regardless of your roadblock, there is always a way to resolve it. Sometimes it means being industrious. Other times it means making many changes. At the bottom of all this is effort—reframing your situation and taking a proactive approach to finding a man.

As you can see, the only excuse for being single is your lack of initiative. If your excuse is that you can't afford a baby-sitter, arrange with another single mom to swap baby-sitting nights to absorb child care expenses. Being single also can't be blamed on the lack of good men. The fact that you are not looking in the places quality men frequent is the problem. This list can go on and on. Until you stop blaming and take responsibility for yourself, nothing will change in your life. You will remain single or continue settling for less than you deserve. Now is the time to look at your roadblocks differently and overcome them. Once you do, you will be on your way to finding a man for you.

Getting Rid of the Roadblocks

As you've learned, roadblocks come in many forms. My goal is to help you recognize the reasons you are not meeting your ideal man. Once you recognize the reasons, then it's time to learn how to eliminate the roadblocks. The goal of this book is to get rid of unnecessary roadblocks by teaching you skills to overcome the hurdles. That will put you in a new arena where you'll come in contact with the type of men you desire.

Dear Diary . . .

The man I had a date with tonight can only be categorized as a reject. I'm 5'1" and he towered over me with one-and-a half feet of uncontrollable body parts!

The goodnight kiss proved painful. A pain in the neck, you might say. The problem was not the disparity in our heights. No, it was in the difference in opinion as to where his hands should be.

Without permission, his hands went north. No, no, bad boy. Giving him the benefit of the doubt, I placed them back on my waist. Ignoring my lack of interest, his hands traveled south. Creep. It's time to go home.

No dessert for the naughty boy who couldn't listen. This should teach him how to treat a girl. This girl only plays with boys who get permission first.

———————

3

Types of Attraction

Women often find themselves attracted to certain types of men. Attraction can be broken down into two aspects: physical and emotional. The foundation of attraction is developed in adolescence. This is a time in which separation from the parents begins and an assessment of unmet needs is explored. Society teaches girls to fulfill their deficiencies through mates. So the girls go out, seeking mates to fulfill the needs their parents weren't able to meet.

What's interesting about mate selection is that it is narcissistic in nature. People are born with varying degrees of survival skills and have an innate motivation to fulfill unmet needs for the basis of survival. The deeper the deprivation, the stronger the motivation to fill the void. These unmet needs don't disappear as a woman becomes an adult. Instead, the woman searches for a mate to fill the needs for her. As a child, the goal of meeting the need was for life survival. As adult women, these same unmet needs transform into an emotional void.

At this point, you are probably wondering what the basic categories of needs are and which areas you may have a deficit in. The mystery is about to be disclosed. Here you will find categories of typical emotional reactions to unmet needs. Circle all the feelings that you have felt over the last six months. Doing this exercise will help you recognize which of your needs are unmet. (See page 16.)

Basic Needs and the Emotion
Created When There Is a Deficiency

Physical Need (When Unmet)	Emotional Needs (When Unmet)
1. Nourishment (deprived)	1. Protection (fear, anxiety)
2. Affection (abandoned)	2. Acceptance (rejection)
3. Shelter (vulnerable)	3. Independence (smothered)

Following the order of this chart, I will begin with a detailed breakdown of the physical side of needs and attraction. A discussion of emotional needs will follow.

Physical Need 1: Nourishment

Nourishment consists of the basic needs for survival, including plenty of healthy food, water, sleep, and air. When any one of these is unmet, the person develops a longing for the missing element. Take, for instance, the girl who grew up poor and never had adequate supplies of her basic needs. In her adult life, those needs manifest as unmet emotional needs. She has emotional hunger; searches for someone to take care of her; is only interested in herself; views men in terms of what they can give her; and is demanding, impatient, envious, jealous, rageful, empty, mistrustful, pessimistic, tired, and depressed because she feels empty. She searches for mates who are capable of supplying what she missed out on as a child. She may seek men in professions who are perceived as givers. These may be chefs, doctors, social workers, psychologists, and teachers.

Physical Need 2: Affection

Affection is physical touching by a loved one that expresses care for a person. Research shows that babies who don't receive enough physical contact waste away and die. When a girl lacks affection, she grows up into a woman who feels rejected, abandoned, unloved, depressed, lonely, hurt, excluded, discouraged, worthless, destroyed, crushed, hopeless, hateful, forsaken, and miserable. In her search for love, she will look for a man who demonstrates his attention in a physical way, through touching her. She may look for men who have careers which involve the expression of touch—artists, hair dressers, or massage therapists. Many of these women get into a paradoxical trap of offering sex to any man who wants it from her. This kind of contact is only temporary because the primary focus is sexual rather than emotional.

Physical Need 3: Shelter

As children, we think of shelter representing a home, a place where there is stability, constancy, predictability, pleasure, and permanency. When a girl is put in the situation in which there is a lot of upheaval as in the case of having to move often, she grows up into a woman who never has a sense of home or roots; feels ungrounded, lost, helpless, mistrustful; maintains emotional distance with men because of her experiences that all people go away; feels unstable and unprotected; is on the alert for danger; is flexible and very adaptable; and craves change.

She looks for a man who offers what she lacked as a child. She will seek someone who has lived in the same area his whole life, a family man to give her a sense of family stability. Overall, she's looking for permanency in a man. She may seek men of the cloth, CPAs, bankers, and those who have a reputation for being stable forces in the community.

Emotional Need 1: Protection

Protection involves a feeling of safety, of knowing that someone is there to cover or shield you from exposure, cruelty, unnecessary pains, injury, or destruction. When protection is lacking, a girl turns into a woman who is either very tough or frail. In either case, underneath, she will be a survivor; maintain emotional distance; and be mistrustful, argumentative, anxious, afraid, insecure, lonely, and stressed.

When looking for a mate, she will look for a man who can take care of her and make her feel safe. She may look for partners who are police officers, fire fighters, weight lifters, and other men who symbolize protection and strength.

Emotional Need 2: Acceptance

Acceptance means being unconditionally accepted by someone significant. Ideally, it means having someone who loves you for who you are and accepts every aspect of your character, even your flaws. Acceptance is shown in a variety of ways: offerings of praise, support, encouragement, and pats on the back for a job well done. The little girl who doesn't feel accepted grows into an adult who doubts the things she does, seeks approval from others, discounts accomplishments, has low self-esteem, fears rejection, feels unworthy and less than others, knocks herself down, and has a low energy level. She seeks men who will praise her talents or point out the good in her. Her goal is to find a man who will worship the ground she walks on. She will be drawn to men who are verbally expressive, and who may work as teachers, public speakers, or entertainers.

Emotional Need 3: Independence

Independence allows a person to explore new environments without being overly restricted. Being guided, not controlled, leads to high self-esteem and confidence in the person's ability to be successful. When a girl is overly controlled and freedom is restricted, she will grow into a woman who experiences the need to rely on others, gives up easily, becomes frustrated quickly, has low self-esteem, feels angry, has a lot of self-doubt, and expects others to do things for her if she gives up.

Her type of man will give her freedom to explore but will always be there to pick her up and put things back together for her. She may be attracted to men who are motivational and

Emotional Responses to Unmet Needs

Fear, Anxiety

afraid	jumpy
agitated	lonely
alarmed	nervous
anxious	overwhelmed
apprehensive	panicky
desperate	restless
embarrassed	shaky
fearful	tense
frightened	terrified
hesitant	uncomfortable
insecure	uneasy
intimidated	

Rejected, Depressed

abandoned	forsaken
alienated	hatred
alone	hopeless
battered	horrible
blue	humiliated
crushed	hurtleft out
defeated	lonesome
despair	ostracized
despised	overlooked
despondent	rejected
destroyed	sad
discouraged	unloved
downhearted	vulnerable
dreadful	worthless
excluded	

Anger

agitated
aggravated
annoyed
enraged
furious
hateful
irritated
mad
oppressed
outraged
resentful
revengeful
spiteful

Weak

flimsy
forceless
frail
impotent
low strength
unequal
unstable

Smothered

anger
asphyxiated
boxed in
choking
held back
helpless
panic
repressed
restricted
stifled
suffocated
suppressed

Deprived

angry
bankrupt
bare
craving
empty
famished
hollow
hungry
impoverished
insatiable
lethargic
lustful
starving
stripped
thirsty
yearning

inspiring. She may also be drawn to overly controlling men who never allow her the freedom to grow.

In exploring the six basic needs, you will find some similarities between the categories of unmet needs. This is because all six of these needs are basic building blocks for life. When one is a little shaky, it makes the rest of the personality less stable.

Review the feelings listed on page 16, and circle all those that you experience regularly. When you finish, add up all the circles in each category. See which category most of your circles are in—this area of deprivation is what fuels your search for a man. Searching for your needs is not a bad thing to do, but it can lead to the end of a relationship if you eventually develop the ability to supply the need for yourself. It is wonderful to be able to satisfy your own needs, but don't delay having a relationship until you make yourself 100 percent whole.

Now I want you to think about past relationships you've had. Did any of these men take away the feelings you circled? Think of your past partners. Did they fill the same need for you each time? The problem with having someone else supply your needs is the fact that the void is never filled. Instead, it will resurface when the relationship ends. You will then be in a place of having an unmet need and an overwhelming desire to find someone else to fill it.

When a woman chooses a partner because he fills an unmet need, the relationship will be driven by a childlike emotional immaturity. This only perpetuates the real problems that continue to lie underneath the Band-Aid partner. Sure, the needs are met, but the adult relationship has no real foundation for the couple. As many women can attest, when their needs are met by someone else in a long-term relationship, it gives them the strength to grow emotionally. This relationship replaces the role of the parent and eventually divides the couple because of the woman's emotional stability. She now has adult maturity and is driven away from the parent relationship to find an adult relationship. This is seen very often when a woman changes careers, or goes to college.

Attraction of this sort typically fulfills an unrealistic or un-necessary need based on the past. As you scrutinize your emotional pattern, look for emotional areas that have caused unsatisfying relationships. If the relationships are based on unmet needs, then you need to learn how to fulfill the needs yourself. This book will not discuss how to meet unmet needs, but many others do. You might also consider counseling as another approach to helping you grow.

Next you will read about the aspects of attraction. When I finish describing what each of these aspects mean, you will see a pattern emerge about your need-based attraction. This will help you understand how your pattern of attraction leads you to follow a path of repetition with the wrong type of man for you.

Physical Attraction

Attraction isn't always based on a deficiency in needs. Sometimes it is based on a physical or emotional attraction to a person. *Physical attraction* is the outward characteristics of a man that appeal to a woman. Women are visual in nature less often than men, so they place less importance on a man's physical composition. However, sometimes women are attracted to a physical type. A physical type can be healthy and lead to happy relationships. Other times, women find that they are consistently drawn to a man who is not good for them. Take, for example, Carrie, who is attracted to men who are 5'4" with a husky physique because she grew up with a father who had that shape. This attraction is based on a fond childhood association. The opposite can be the case for the woman who finds herself attracted to a physical type of man who abused her as a child. For example, one of my clients, Mary, was attracted to beautiful men with perfect bodies. After some counseling, she disclosed to me that she had been sexually molested by her softball coach as a child. Coincidentally, his physical description fit that of the men she now found attractive as an adult. She rarely had relationships with these perfect men, and when she did, they paralleled the dynamics of that surreptitious one-sided relationship she had with her coach. She felt that each man's focus was on sex, not on lovemaking. It was also kept secretive, which felt bad to her. The third component that matched the earlier feelings with the coach was her feeling of dirtiness after each sexual encounter. After extensive psychotherapy, Mary realized that she was reenacting a destructive and damaging childhood experience that impacted her adult relationships with men. She was attempting to redo an earlier experience to create a new ending. Unfortunately, she was caught up in a repetitive cycle that ended similarly with each man. In the end, she saw that her physical attraction was not for the actual men she met. Instead, it had to do with unfinished business she was now aware of.

Another variation of a physical attraction comes from Susan. She grew up in a sports-minded family and learned to enjoy spectator sports. She wasn't athletic herself and needed to lose 35 pounds. Since she spent a fair amount of time at sporting events, she tended to date athletic men. It may not come as a surprise, but these men were physically very fit, unlike Susan. She was impressed by their shapes and felt proud to have a Greek god by her side. However, as time passed she found herself angered by their attempts to get her to lose weight. She explained each breakup as being caused by the men nagging her to change her eating style and pressuring her to exercise.

A final example of physical attraction is that experienced by Beverly. She loved men in uniform, especially military men. Right off the bat I assumed the problems she may have came from her past relationships, and I was right. She put it like this: "Well, in the beginning he aggressively pursued me. As time passed he became emotionally distant and spent more time with the 'boys' than with me." He went from aggressive to controlling, attentive to distant, and responsive to emotionally unavailable. I am not claiming that all men who fit the physical description of a uniformed man will have these negative characteristics. What I am saying is that most physical types of men will have a higher probability of displaying the stereotypical characteristics of the group they fall into.

The physical type a woman chooses may be harmless and lead to a happy relationship. However, some women, like Mary, find that they are consistently drawn to a physical type of man who is not good for them.

Emotional Attraction

The second type of attraction is an emotional attraction. Some women find that they don't have a particular physical type of man they are attracted to. However, they may notice that their pattern is a similar feeling they experience with each relationship. This type of attraction is more common and explains the initial attraction most women have toward men. This is the more difficult aspect of attraction to identify because it isn't always apparent.

Diana met Wayne through the personal ads. He sounded appealing in print, so she called him and left a message. Weeks later he returned her call. She felt thankful to have a man calling her, so she excused his tardiness. After each phone call she felt anxious from trying to make him like her. She didn't like the way she felt or acted with him, yet she scheduled their first date. Finally, it dawned on her that she felt the same uncomfortable feelings around Wayne as she did around her father. Diana decided right then and there to stop repeating her emotional pattern. She called Wayne and canceled their date. He berated her for doing so, which further confirmed that he was bad for her. Through her own self-exploration, she realized that she had the strength to stand up for herself and say no. She learned that she was attracted to people who were emotionally abusive because that was all she knew. And for Diana, this pattern of attraction had repeated in the form of an emotional attraction to men. Once she realized what was going on, she found herself emotionally attracted to men who were much kinder.

Do you know your emotional pattern? Do you even have one? Diana learned what hers was when she suddenly had insight into the reason she was attracted to men. Sometimes people discover theirs; other times they choose not to. There is no need to understand emotional attractions if you find your life and relationships fulfilling.

Attractions are complex, and the reason behind the attraction is even more complicated. I once heard a woman say, "When I was 20, love was easy. I fell in love with a man I thought was handsome and he thought I was pretty. We got married. Why can't it be that easy now?" Young love is idealistic and filled with ignorance and denial. Adult love is a different matter altogether. Women discover that past choices haven't been the right choices. Suddenly they realize that they are repeating patterns that are doing more bad than good for them.

As you can see, the physical type of a man that a woman chooses may be good for you, as in Carrie's case. Other times, as with Susan and Mary, she is consistently drawn to a type of man who is not good for her. In the next chapter, you will be asked to think about your type of man in terms of his physical and emotional attraction. At that time you will gain insight into why you choose the men you do and how to make the changes necessary for a happy relationship.

Dear Diary . . .

She looks so pretty! Her makeup and hair and the sexy lingerie she wears, highlighted by the lighting and camera angle are oh so flattering! My boyfriend is not only hand-some, he's pretty!

His disclosure did not go over well. I'm the laughingstock of my friends and family. The marriage proposal which fol-lowed didn't fare much better. Who would wear the wedding gown, anyway?

What was he thinking when he showed me the pictures? Was I to be amused? Accepting? Aroused!

I should have listened to the secret nicknames my friends gave him—"The Homo," and "Mr. Fancy Pants." Let's not forget about the latest one, "Mr. Transvestite!" How will I ever date again?

4

Evaluating Past Relationships

Many women are unable to describe which emotional and/or physical characteristics attract them to men. The goal of this chapter is to help you recognize red flags in a potential relationship, so that you can avoid repeating past mistakes. Relationship mistakes are typically based on emotional shortcomings from childhood, which you read about in the previous chapter. As adults, women strive to fulfill these maintained deprivations through the mates they choose.

Reasons to Know Your Type

It is important for a woman to know what she desires, for three reasons:

1. Women are typically attracted to the same type of man in each relationship. This is fine if that type leads to a healthy relationship that meets the woman's needs. However, if a woman continually finds herself in unsatisfying relationships, something isn't working. The woman needs to understand what it is about these men that she finds attractive but is at the same time destructive.

2. Evaluating your past relationships allows you to see which basic needs you are trying to meet in your relationships with men. Before continuing with this chapter, review Chapter 3, "Types of Attraction," which teaches you how to evaluate which basic needs drive you to choose your mates.

3. Time flies! Don't waste your time with the wrong type of man. Keep in mind that patterns are like the grooves on a record. Old records (relationship patterns) tend to have scratches that cause the needle to stick, creating an ugly repetitive noise rather than enjoyable music. The only thing that creates beautiful music is to pick up the needle and put it on a new groove. This requires effort on your part. You have to be the one to make the decision to change (pick up the needle) because no one else will make it for you. Thinking about making changes is easy to do. Making the changes is the hard part. Being stuck in a groove doesn't always sound good, but it's comfortable because it requires too much effort to move it.

Evaluating the Past

For this section, you will need a blank notebook to complete the upcoming exercises. On the top of a blank page, write the title "Evaluating the Past" (see the example). This will be your reference page to help stimulate memories of your past relationships. On that page, tape pictures of men from your last three significant relationships. Go ahead—pull out your photo albums, dig through your drawers, do whatever you have to do. But do find the pictures to put in your notebook. Memory tends to distort a person's perceptions of what the men looked like, who they were, and how they treated you. By looking at actual pictures, reality will be more accurately recalled.

Norma said that her men were all so different until she taped their pictures into her notebook. It had never dawned on her that they all had a devilish charm about their appearances. They had dimples on their cheeks, sexy poses, and similar "bad

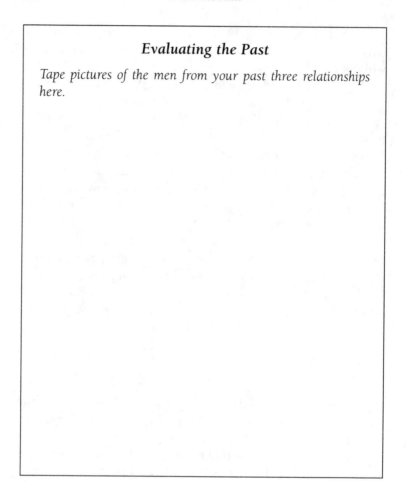

Evaluating the Past

Tape pictures of the men from your past three relationships here.

boy" haircuts with one side of their bangs hanging over one eye. That was the type of man that was attractive to her.

Physical Type

Listed here are various physical characteristics to help you describe men. Fill in the blanks with the descriptions of the men from your last three significant relationships. Remember to refer to the first page of your notebook with the actual pictures.

	Man 1	Man 2	Man 3
Weight			
Height			
Race			
Hair color			
Hair length			
Hairstyle			
Age range			
Eye color			
Nose shape			
Style of jewelry			
Style of dress			
Eyeglasses or not			
Body shape			
Dimples			
Suntan or not			

According to this list, do you have a physical type of man that you are attracted to each time? Describe that pattern here:

_____

_____

_____

Emotional Type

List the names of the men with whom you had your past three relationships:

Man 1_____

Man 2_____

Man 3_____

Think about one man at a time. As you remember the man, write down what initially attracted you to him:

Man 1_____

Man 2_____

Man 3_____

Answer the following questions as completely as possible. The more insight you have into what motivates your attraction to the type of men who attract you, the faster you can break your faulty mate selection pattern.

QUESTION 1

What basic physical needs, if any, did each man supply for you? If none of your basic needs were met, try to remember whether there were any physical needs you originally saw each man as being able to supply. The basic needs are listed here. Refer to the previous chapter for the definition of each need. Fill in all that apply:

Nourishment need_____

Affection need_____

Shelter need_____

QUESTION 2

Do you see any common patterns in the physical type of men you are attracted to?

_____

_____

_____

QUESTION 3

If you have a physical attraction pattern, does this person resemble someone from your past? If so, what kind of resemblance is it, and what was your relationship to that person? Remember to incorporate what basic need or needs that person provided for you. If that person didn't provide a basic need for you, did a need go unmet?

_____

_____

_____

QUESTION 4

Think of each man in terms of the basic needs again. This time the focus should be in terms of emotional needs. List each emotional need that was met by each man or what you expected each to provide.

Protection need_____

Acceptance need_____

Independence need_____

In one sentence or less, write down the cause of your past breakups with each man:

Man 1_____

Man 2_____

Man 3_____

Most women discover that the main problem in a relationship is based on the characteristics that they initially found attractive. As you will recall, women tend to be attracted to men who possess the need they lack. For example, Amy felt as though she was never given the chance to make her own choices. She became a librarian to make her mother happy. When she met Matt, she was attracted to his free lifestyle of being in a band. She admired his ability to be independent because she lacked this aspect in her own life. However, after four months the attraction began to dry up. Her life as a librarian consisted of early mornings, a lot of structure, and consistency. Matt's antithetical lifestyles eventually led to conflict with hers. Consequently, their relationship broke up because of a lifestyle she at one time found exciting.

Another example is that of Annette. She was attracted to men who did not have their own careers, so that they could be a great source of support for her endeavors. However, she discovered that these men had no interests of their own, which made for boring interactions. In the end, her relationships ended because of the original thing she found attractive.

Another Piece to the Puzzle

Try to recall the *positive* personal characteristics of the men from your past three relationships. List them:

Man 1_____

Man 2_____

Man 3_____

Keeping the same men in mind, now list their *negative* personal characteristics:

Man 1_____

Man 2_____

Man 3_____

Your Role in the Relationship

Okay, we've concentrated enough on the role men played in the relationships. Now evaluate how you may have contributed negatively to the relationships. Remember, it takes two people to make and break a partnership. You can do it. If you have to, pretend that you are describing your "friend's" past relationships. Describe in one sentence how you contributed to the past breakups:

Man 1_____

Man 2_____

Man 3_____

A relationship has so many dynamics. Some are more important than others. In this chapter, I have covered the foundation of what makes a relationship fail or succeed. By learning which area you have had difficulties in, you can concentrate your efforts on repairing the flawed area within yourself.

Dear Diary . . .

Sure, I have qualities that I'm looking for in a man. I don't even think my standards are unrealistic. I've dated several men lately, and none of them fit the bill. Tom smoked like a chimney. Jim wanted to add me to his harem collection. Todd loved secrets, especially keeping his wife from finding out about me. Now, Ken was just right except for the fact that getting together involved five hours of flight, two plane changes, and several hours of traveling by car. I'm persistent. I'll keep trying. I have four blind dates this week: a doctor, lawyer, merchant, and Indian chief. I should like one of them!

5

Defining the Right Man for You

At age three, girls begin to fill their minds with images of the perfect man as they listen to stories of Cinderella and Prince Charming. Life can sometimes shatter your fantasy man when your first boyfriend is more like the infamous Rumpelstiltskin. You shake your head in bewilderment as you ask, "How could this have happened?"

The Delusional Man

Now, as an adult, it is time to once again describe your ideal fairy-tale prince. Take some time—think about your needs, desires, and the type of man who can make you happy. When selecting a compatible partner, consider three aspects:

1. Physical
2. Emotional
3. Miscellaneous

When describing a man, these are the three areas that make up a whole individual. You must take all three into consideration, or you will be overlooking crucial elements in your ideal man. In the next sections you will find each of the areas broken down into detail. Take your time as you consider each aspect and what is "right" for you. Remember, your goal is to find a man with whom you will have a happy relationship.

Physical Aspects of Creating a Mate

Here you will find the physical aspects of your ideal man, broken down into detail. Fill in the blanks according to how you would like your Prince Charming to look:

Weight_____

Height_____

Race_____

Hair color_____

Hair length/style_____

Age range_____

Eye color_____

Nose shape_____

Style of jewelry_____

Style of clothes_____

Eyeglasses or not_____

Body shape_____

Dimples_____

Suntan or not_____

Emotional Aspects of Creating a Mate

Here you will find the emotional aspects of a man broken down into detail. Fill in the blanks according to how you would like your him to be. Remember, you want to focus on the emotional aspect only. You are creating the man of your dreams, the one you keep hoping to find. You don't have to settle for less. So write what you need a man to have.

Personality type _____
                    (introverted / extroverted / in between)

Hobbies_____

Skills_____

Talents _____

Sexual interest: strong_____ moderate_____ secondary_____

Indoor or outdoor type_____

Able to articulate feelings_____

Spirituality_____

Religion_____

TV watcher_____

Sense of humor_____

Independent_____

Needy_____

Romantic_____

Sensitive_____

Argumentative_____

Intelligent_____

Likes: pets_____ children_____ music_____

movies_____ theater_____ sports _____

Other emotional aspects_____

Miscellaneous Aspects of Creating a Mate

Here you will find the extraneous aspects of men. This category
is broken down into detail to allow you to see which characteristics are important to you. Typically women overlook this
category in the mate selection process. As I said earlier, all aspects are important if you want to find a suitable partner.

Fill in the blanks according to how you would create
your mate.

Educational level_____

Type of job_____

Lifestyle_____

Values_____

Attitude about life_____

Goals_____

Conversationalist (yes/no)_____

Children (yes/no)_____

Past marriage (okay or not)_____

Smoker_____

Alcohol use:
   social_____ moderate _____ none_____

Health conscious (yes/no)_____ food_____ physical activity_____

Other variables_____

Analysis of Your Ideal Man

Imagine the man you have created. Go through all of the characteristics again and keep them in mind. As you think about the man you desire, ask yourself the following questions:

QUESTION 1

Who does this ideal man bring to mind?

A celebrity_____

Someone you looked up to_____

Someone you once had a crush on_____

A teacher/professor_____

Your father_____

QUESTION 2

Does your ideal man physically or emotionally resemble a man with whom you had a past relationship?

  ☐ Yes (In what way?)_____

  ☐ No (Why not?)_____

Although no surprise, most women continually find themselves attracted to similar types of men in each relationship. Are they perpetuating the same relationship, the only difference being that he has a different name and a different background?

Was your past relationship good? If it was, fine. Find a new relationship just like that. However, if it was bad and the characteristics that you created in your ideal man fit that same man, ask yourself, "Why do I want to repeat the same relationship?" If you keep up that pattern, each relationship will end for the same reasons.

Categorizing Men's Characteristics

If you have been reading this book in sequence, you should have a good idea of the characteristics you want a man to have. If you are like most women, you probably prefer some characteristics over others. I want you to begin to think of those characteristics in three categories:

1. *Must be*—These are qualities that a mate must have for you to be happy.
2. *Can't tolerate*—These qualities are destructive to a relationship. They lead to low self-esteem and resentment.
3. *Possible compromise*—The qualities in this group are not bad qualities. It is simply a matter of reframing overlooked qualities in terms of being acceptable.

To further demonstrate what I am discussing, I am going to describe Cindy's situation. She is a 41-year-old single mother who has been divorced for seven years. When I asked Cindy to develop a list of qualities, she knew exactly what she wanted. She was also clear on what she didn't want. Here is a shortened list of what she came up with:

Must Be	Can't Tolerate	Possible Compromise
Generous	Alcohol drinker	
Faithful	Short men	
Health conscious	Overweight	
Dependable	Men with children	
Reliable	Smothering	
Even tempered	Jealous	
Athletic	Smoker	
Spiritual	Workaholic	

Must Be	Can't Tolerate	Possible Compromise
Sexual	Introverts	
Passionate	Bald men	
Attentive	Nonprofessional	
Intelligent	Aggressive	
Honest	Arrogant	
Financially secure	Skinny men	
Mature	Older than 45	
Educated	Womanizer	

According to Cindy, her ideal type of man must be 6'2", dark hair, light eyes, nice complexion, manly looking, hairy chest, interested in her, a one-woman man, honest, and with a muscular body. I asked her to really look at the "Can't Tolerate" column to see whether some of those qualities were actually acceptable. She laughed in disbelief at some of her answers. Cindy's revised list of "Possible Compromise" characteristics:

Smoker

Short men

Divorced men

Men with children

Bald men

Nonprofessional men

No older than 55

Thin but not skinny

Cindy learned that she could be just as attracted to a different type of man if he possessed many of the emotional characteristics she needed to make her happy. Because of this alteration, her range of potential mates increased when she decided to be more flexible in terms of what she would accept in a partner. Originally, she had listed all of the "Possible Compromise" items in the "Can't Tolerate" column. After thinking about each characteristic, she began to realize that her reasoning behind the "Can't Tolerate" column was based on what her mother had told her to avoid. She began to wonder why she was still trying to please her mother. She decided to start think-ing about herself and what she wanted.

Cindy ended up dating and being very happy with a man who she once wouldn't have given the time of day to. That's the whole point of reconsidering the qualities you could "possibly compromise" on. Mate selection isn't about pleasing others or idealism—it's about finding a partner to be happy with.

Diamonds in the Rough

Sometimes women, such as Cindy, discard or overlook a po-tential relationship because a man may have one characteristic they do not like. The characteristic may not be a terrible one, but it prevents the women from recognizing a real gem of a man. Ask yourself whether you can compromise. For instance, I am frequently asked the question "I am attracted to a man who has a slight punctuality (attentiveness, fashion, weight, etc.) problem. How can I get him to be on time (pay more at-tention, dress better, lose weight, etc.)?" My answer is always the same: "You can't. You have to either accept his constantly being 15 minutes late or find a partner who values punctual-ity." This is called a compromise. Can you overlook one un-attractive aspect of a man (such as being 15 minutes late) and see less obvious characteristics that are very attractive?

Beauty and the Beast

With all the discussion about compromising, a fairy tale comes to mind, "The Beauty and the Beast." If you remember, the beauty decided to overlook the ugliness of the beast. Once she did that, she found true love. She eventually came to notice and appreciate the more subtle, attractive aspects of the beast. She compromised!

Now it's your turn. Fill in the three categories here with the qualities that apply. Most women tend to think of a man's char-acteristics in two terms: "must have" and "can't tolerate." Such dichotomous thinking tends to lessen the pool of potential partners. The most important part of this sheet is the last category, "Possible Compromise." By adding this group it allows you to think beyond an idealistic and unattainable partner. Don't interpret the last category as "settling for less" because it isn't. It is simply being more open-minded.

NEWLY ACQUIRED TASTES IN MEN

Must Be	Can't Tolerate	Possible Compromise
_____	_____	_____
_____	_____	_____
_____	_____	_____
_____	_____	_____
_____	_____	_____
_____	_____	_____
_____	_____	_____
_____	_____	_____

An interesting study done by *Health & Mind* magazine (November 1994) reveals what men and women rank as their ideal qualities in a partner. Men first looked for attractiveness, followed by personality, age, interests/activities, with the least concern being weight. Women, on the other hand, first looked for an ideal partner who had a great personality, then had shared or similar interests/activities, attitudes, attractiveness, and last age. Do you agree with their findings? By the time you finish this chapter, you should know what your top five qualities are too.

Dear Diary . . .
   Hindsight demarcated the truth. He followed the classic gold-digger script. Preying on my weakness, he sought future security . . . in money he imagined I had. Imagine that.

Yes, I'm well off. I live in a well-to-do neighborhood—in a rented apartment! I have great transportation—the tow-truck driver tells me each week as he carts it away. I dine in the most expensive restaurants—thanks to my dates who treat me like a queen. Diamonds are a girl's best friend; mine sits in a pawn shop—I keep hoping it will be next month's rent.

With my ego still bruised from last night's date, I sit in silk pajamas sipping gourmet coffee. Glancing down, the top magazine warns of men to avoid. Imagine that. I do need to keep up on my readings.

———————

6

Men to Avoid

Do you find yourself getting into relationships that aren't meeting your needs? A lot of women do. The first step to changing this is to identify what your "pattern" is. You have to identify the type of man you are attracted to. Is he married? Is he too dependent? Is he abusive? What is he?

What Type of Men Should Be Avoided?

There are all sorts of men to avoid because they cause more pain than pleasure. This chapter lumps the more common types of men together to make identifying them easier when you meet them. You will learn how to identify men who are married, abusive, emotionally dependent, on the rebound, gold diggers, and noncommitters. A relationship with any one of these types is destined to fail. Many women spend months and years trying to salvage a relationship with someone who isn't capable of having one.

If you've had a lot of these relationships, then you definitely have a pattern of getting involved with the wrong type of man. The sooner a woman sees the early warning signs, the sooner she can end the relationship and move on to one that can be successful. The end of the chapter will give you the profile of the best kind of men for healthy relationships: committers who are psychologically healthy.

Men who should be avoided have two common features. First, having a relationship with any of them is bound to give you a heartache. These are the men who are incapable of giving 50 percent to make the relationship work. As a matter of fact, most of them view the relationship in terms of what's in it for them and offer nothing. The second commonality for most of these men is an abusive cycle. This pattern can be emotional, not necessarily physical, and leads to damaged self-esteem for the woman. The end result for all of these types is emotional exhaustion for the woman and a failed relationship for both.

The Married Man

Who are the women that get involved with married men? Are they desperate losers? Absolutely not! They are women just like you—normal and productive. Between 5 and 20 percent of all single women over the age of 35 will have an ongoing relationship with a married man.

Women sometimes feel that they are too old (38+) to find a man. Because of this, they feel as though they need to "settle" for whoever comes along, even if this means he's married. Another reason a woman may get involved with a married man is due to her fear of commitments. She is afraid a man will abandon her so she chooses a man who can't have her anyway so he never rejects her. Both of these women compromise their needs by allowing the married man to dictate their lives and hearts. The outcome is almost always the same: no marriage and a broken heart.

The sad thing about being involved with a married man is the fact that the woman is settling for less. She is settling for not being a priority in the man's life. The only way a woman is able to tolerate her inferior status in this situation is by being accommodating and having unusually strong self-esteem.

Screening for an Undisclosed Married Man

Sometimes a woman has no idea that a man is married when she begins dating him. By the time she discovers the truth, her emotional bond is hard to break. Listed here are signs to look for when you meet a man to help you discover whether he is married. The more signs you check off, the more likely it is that he has a wife.

1. He avoids conversation about marriage.
2. You have no way to reach him by phone in the evenings or on weekends.
3. He lies to you regularly.
4. He gets angry when you send gifts to his place of employment.
5. He says that he has separated from his wife but can't file for divorce because the time isn't right or some other vague reason.
6. He doesn't introduce you to any of his friends or relatives.
7. He denies having children but later admits that he does.
8. Once you set up a date, you can't depend on him to show up.
9. He never invites you to his home.
10. He doesn't want you to call him at work.
11. Time spent together is all-consuming and intense.
12. If the two of you run into someone he knows, he becomes aloof.
13. He complains about how neglectful his "ex-wife" was and how good you make him feel.
14. He sets strict rules about your relationship.
15. He can rarely see you for longer than three hours at a time.
16. He will avoid weekend dates, especially Saturday night.
17. He avoids details about his life.
18. His courting is pushy rather than romantic.

"Gwen" and "Craig"

Gwen dated Craig for two months before she discovered that he was married. He courted her with flowers, cards, phone calls, and weekend dates. She started to become suspicious the night he brought her back to his studio apartment for an "evening of fun." None of his belongings seemed to fit his personality, and she couldn't understand why he and his roommate shared a bed. She was so put off by his centerfold posters that she had him take her home before things got out of hand. Two weeks later, Gwen received a phone call from Craig's wife, and was informed that Craig had gonorrhea, and twelve other lovers.

The Abusive Man

The typical profile of a woman who gets involved with an abusive man is someone who came from an abusive family herself. These men are usually attracted to her lack of self-worth because they know that she will put up with being mistreated. Because she is used to tumultuous relationships like this, she is unable to see the nuances of trouble. When she finally knows it's an abusive relationship, it is because the problems have escalated to a dangerous level. Sometimes she's not always aware of the signs until actual physical abuse takes place or extreme mental cruelty occurs. An abusive man uses charm to attract a woman. Later it's another story when he uses intimidation to control her, devalues her worth, makes her feel guilty, and reveals many other bad qualities.

Becky and Steve had been dating for only two weeks before they took a trip to New York together. Steve was a silent, manly type of man, who had lots of muscles. He lived a pretty isolated life and had no real interests other than traveling and spending his millions and millions of dollars. When Becky looked at Steve, she saw a needy, sad little boy inside, and she wanted to give him love. After the first time they made love, she thought it was unusual when he put the sheet between their bodies to block the intimacy of skin contact. Steve's true colors came out the second day of the trip when he took Becky shopping at a designer store. He had everyone waiting on them, and when she was really enjoying herself, he said, "Don't get used to this, babe—this is my lifestyle, not yours." When the purchase was delivered to the hotel, he became enraged when one item of the outfit was missing. In his rage, the outfit was sent back rather than having the store drop off the missing item. The intimacy that had developed was stripped away with insults and other negatives. To top things off, Steve put Becky on a plane back home while he flew off to Europe with another woman. The relationship was over.

As with Becky's story, the symptoms occur in a cyclical pattern beginning with the honeymoon phase when everything is wonderful. He's charming and loving and enjoyable to be around. The next stage is when the tension builds up through screaming, yelling, blaming, demanding, and sometimes engaging in mild forms of shoving or rape-style sex. When the abuse is emotional in nature, insults, guilt trips, and emotional injury begin. The third stage is the explosion of anger when something triggers the violent event. In Becky's case, it was the store's forgetfulness. After the outburst, the man gets frightened that his girlfriend or wife will leave him, plus he feels guilty for overreacting, setting in motion the honeymoon stage all over again as a way of winning her love back.

Screening for an Abusive Man

The following list encompasses qualities that are characteristic of abusive men. If your pattern is getting involved with men of this nature, then you need to train yourself to recognize these early warning signs. If you answer yes to the following questions, then you need to pay attention to the warnings for your own safety and happiness:

1. Does he criticize some of your good qualities?
2. Does he have an abusive or criminal background?
3. Do you have a lower self-image after being with him?
4. Does he have a drinking or drug problem?
5. Do his emotions run like a roller coaster?
6. Does he try to keep you from becoming more successful?
7. Does he become jealous easily?
8. Did his father abuse his mother?
9. Does his brother abuse his girlfriend or wife?
10. Does he always want to know where you're going, where you've been, want an explanation if you're running late? Do you have to check in with him regularly?

11. Does he refuse to listen to or value your opinions?
12. Does he violate the rights of others?
13. Is he irresponsible?
14. Does he lack loyalty or the formation of enduring relationships?
15. Does he mind your spending time alone or with friends? Do your friends and family dislike him?
16. Does he persistently lie?
17. Is he impulsive?
18. Does he refuse to respect your decision about birth control?
19. Does he have a history of truancy, delinquency, and running away?
20. Does he consistently point out your faults rather than compliment you on your achievements?
21. Does he express affection easily?
22. Does he justify a man's right to strike his wife under certain circumstances?
23. When he gets upset, does he throw or break things?
24. Does he blame others for his problems?

Emotionally Dependent Men

The traditional definition of a man implies strength. However, some men have a dependency problem that is equivalent to weakness. A little bit of dependency can be nice, but a lot can be smothering, which is destructive to a relationship. These men are also highly sensitive and insecure and believe that every man wants you as much as they do.

At age 42, Sandy finally met the man of her dreams, Jon. He had recently divorced and moved three states away from his ex-wife to start life over, and that's when he met Sandy. As the weeks went by, Jon became very insecure of Sandy's love for him because her job exposed her to single people. It got to a point where he needed so much reassurance that it was unbearable to even be with him. He eventually drove her away when he began to accuse her of cheating on him. Enough was enough.

Screening for an Emotionally Dependent Man

If you have a pattern of getting involved with men who live their lives through you, then you need to read this page. If a man has several of the points listed here, that is a red flag. You should pay attention to the warnings to stop repeating unsatisfying relationship patterns.

1. The focus of his life is external.
2. He makes you feel guilty when you choose not to be with him.
3. He is highly sensitive.
4. He requires nonending attention.
5. His life is always filled with emotional chaos that you need to help with.
6. He seems to have a drive to appear better off than others, including close friends and family.
7. He becomes jealous easily.
8. He has a high level of insecurity.
9. He doesn't have any long-term friendships.
10. His job history is erratic, never being able to stay employed long term.
11. He is very sensitive to criticism.
12. You feel as though you are walking on broken glass, always afraid to say the wrong thing so you don't upset him.
13. He has bad family relationships.
14. He is afraid of being rejected or abandoned.
15. He always seems to have an emotional void that can't be filled.
16. He has a history of seeing therapists.
17. He blames others for all that goes wrong in his life.
18. As long as he is the focus of your attention, he is happy.
19. He is notorious for canceling plans at the last minute.
20. You can't rely on him.
21. He never disagrees with you, shares all your interests, and at first may seem like your ideal man because he is a mirror of you.

22. He has a streak of meanness toward others for no reason, especially those he views as a threat to his relationship with you.
23. He is highly reactive.
24. He is threatened by all relationships you have with men.

If a woman decides she can handle a man's dependency, she needs to follow a few guidelines. She will have to schedule specific time with the man and never break the dates because this will exacerbate symptoms. Setting firm boundaries with these men is also a must.

Men on the Rebound

Men on the rebound can usually be found in bars every night. They feel desperately alone and are looking for a woman to replace the one that just got away. Having a relationship with this kind of man is great in the beginning because he's so attentive and appreciative to have you around. Things go so smoothly that you may be fooled into thinking he's your soul mate. Soon, things begin to change as his wounds from his last relationship begin to surface. That is the turning point in which the woman feels more like a therapist doing crisis counseling than a partner in a relationship.

The woman usually ends the relationship when she feels emotionally depleted.

Screening for a Man
on the Rebound

Here are traits characterizing a man still suffering from a past relationship. Be alert to them now to avoid heartache later.

1. He is very adaptable to your lifestyle and interest and aims to please you.
2. He gives too much, too soon.
3. Long-term plans are made early on.
4. He shows extreme neediness.

5. He is overly romantic.
6. He makes threats of possible suicide if you were to leave him.
7. Premature plans are made to have a family together to replace the one he left (if he's newly divorced).
8. He acts helpless to his surroundings.
9. He needs a caretaker.
10. He's an emotional basket case.
11. His apartment is bare, which reflects how empty he feels.
12. He wants you to make a home for the two of you.
13. He wants to spend too much time at your house.
14. He tries to mold you into the woman who left him.
15. He's been out of his relationship less than one year.
16. He plays the wounded victim and feels sorry for himself.
17. Many times these men are impotent because of emotional stresses.
18. He wants you to listen to his endless stories about his ex.
19. He needs a lot of sympathy from you.
20. He needs a lot of reassurance that you won't leave him too.
21. He's anxious and worries a lot.
22. He sings your praises and treats you like a queen.

Gold Diggers

This may seem like an unusual category to put in a book for women; however, many women experience men who try to take advantage of them financially. A gold digger is a man who is only attracted to women who are financially able to buy their attention. This can happen to women from all income levels. The key element of attraction is a steady income so the man can pay his bills. These men see women as a blank check with no limit. When a woman has a relationship with a gold digger, the only need of hers that gets met is her sexual appetite. He does his duty to keep her happy and spends her money to make him happy. This kind of relationship can exist for a while when both people are happy, but a time comes when the woman wants her emotional needs met and the man can't deliver.

Screening for a Gold Digger

These are the indications of a gold digger:

1. He's charming.
2. He's suddenly lost his job.
3. He's self-absorbed.
4. He's spontaneous and lots of fun.
5. He has no close friends.
6. He asks to move in with you "temporarily."
7. He apologizes for not being able to pay for things.
8. He will make interesting plans that you end up paying for.
9. He's helpful and full of suggestions.
10. The focus of the relationship is on money and sex.
11. The relationship has a lot of drama and excitement.
12. The woman finds herself buying lots of gifts for the man.
13. He finds a way to drive your car, live in your house, spend your money, and use your credit cards.
14. The woman finds herself paying the man's bills.
15. Very little time is spent getting to know each other emotionally.
16. The man is very demanding and takes charge.
17. He's high maintenance.
18. He's moody.
19. The relationship centers around the man's demands.
20. The woman's sole role in the relationship revolves around her money.
21. The man has a pattern of being in relationships with wealthy women.

The Noncommitting Man

The noncommitting man is the classic "hard-to-get" man. He has no desire to establish a committed relationship with one woman at that particular point in his life.

"Jim" and "Barbara"

Barbara knew that Jim was a charmer, and had a history of promiscuity. However, she assumed that he would eventually make a commitment to her because they got along so well. She was wrong. Instead, within a three-month period, she found love letters from other women, airline tickets with another woman's name, and even caught him in bed with her friend.

Screening for the Noncommitting Man

Listed here are the points that classify a man as unable to make a commitment to women. Mark the points that you recognize. The more points you see in a man, the stronger his fear of commitment to women is.

1. He makes excuses for not being involved in a single relationship.
2. He is always involved with several women.
3. He likes to be entertained rather than spending quiet times together.
4. He never answers his phone in the evenings because he's out chasing skirts.
5. If the phone rings when you are at his house, he lets the answering machine pick it up.
6. You're never sure about plans; you can't depend on his calls.
7. He can't remember details about previous conversations and gets your life facts mixed up with other women's facts.
8. His work seems more important to him than dating.
9. He doesn't put any work into the relationship.
10. He disappears the moment a problem arises.
11. He is not a team player; instead, he's a self-sufficient loner.
12. He seems to get his emotional needs met elsewhere.
13. Time together is spent at your house, not his.
14. When you show less interest in him, he pursues you.

15. He appears to forget you unless you keep the friendship lines open.
16. He's charming and fun to be around.
17. He gets caught telling "white" lies.

Characteristics of Mr. Right

What makes a man Mr. Right is different for every woman. It all depends on what she needs from a man to make her happy. In this chapter, you have learned many warning signs to look for to recognize Mr. Wrong before you get involved with him. In this section you will learn how to find a compatible partner based on a person's emotional makeup as well as the general characteristics to look for in a man who is ready to have a relationship.

Five core emotional aspects make up a person: emotional, sexual, intellectual, financial, and spiritual. For a relationship to work, each person must have the same level of functioning on a rating scale of 1 to 5 in each of the areas. Conflict is inevitable for the couple who has extreme discrepancies in their rankings on the individual core elements. If a man does not closely match your ranking scale, then he will likely end up being too problematic to enjoy.

Use each of the categories here to screen potential mates for comparability. Because this is a new way of looking at a man, I will explain more fully what each element involves.

Core Element 1: Emotional

The first core element in a person's makeup is the emotional aspect. This area includes a person's psychological characteristics along with emotional styles and expressions. This element of a person has its roots in childhood, which forms how a person feels about himself and others. Emotional aspects include:

- Emotional health
- Perspective of the world—cognitive view or emotional outlook
- Opinion of self

- Level of self-esteem
- Feelings of self-worth
- Time put into self-care
- Attitude
- Level of confidence
- Ability to communicate
- How conflict is dealt with
- Importance of others
- Importance of romance
- Ability to commit to a relationship
- Level of intimacy
- Ability to share
- Maturity level
- Sense of openness
- Psychological damage
- Sense of consequences of behaviors
- What is found as rewarding
- Conformity
- Weaknesses
- Strengths
- Respectful to others
- Value of self
- Physical fitness
- Emotional fitness
- Health consciousness
- Vanity
- Narcissism

The list is endless, so add all the qualities that you want to share with a mate.

Core Element 2: Sexual

Sexuality means something different for everyone. For some, it involves having intercourse and a strong sexual attraction. For others the focus is on intimate conversations. As for Heather, she sought partners who were emotionally expressive and romantic, but not particularly sexual. Richard, on the other hand,

was a little on the mischievous side, and wanted a playful partner who wouldn't think twice about sneaking up to a rooftop
after dinner to enjoy a little dessert. Below I've listed various aspects to keep in mind when looking for a partner:

- Sexual expression
- Sexual orientation
- Level of interest in sex
- Intimacy
- Sexual language
- Romance
- Sensitivity
- Playfulness
- Risk taking
- Sexual behaviors
- Love
- Attraction
- Turn-ons
- Sexual variations
- Awareness of sexually transmitted diseases
- Comfort with sexual expression
- Body image
- Sexual lifestyle
- Pregnancy and childbirth
- Commitment
- Monogamy
- Affairs
- Sexual function or dysfunction
- Knowledge of anatomy
- Sexual communication
- Foreplay
- Afterplay
- Celibacy
- Sex toys
- Gender differences
- Physical appearance
- Sexual response

Core Element 3: Intellectual

"Intellectual" refers to how a person thinks about his world and how he interacts in his daily life. People process life's events in various ways. For some, it means being laid-back about life. Others like lots of stimulation and thrive on diversity. A person's intellectual style influences choice of hobbies, sense of humor, and the way someone experiences life on a daily basis. Intellectual style includes:

- Expression of ideas
- Level of education
- Ability to articulate feelings and thoughts
- Sense of humor
- Level of intelligence
- Quickness of thought
- Brightness
- Interests
- Style of interaction
- Type of job
- Goals
- Skills
- Mistakes
- Hobbies
- Knowledge
- Life experiences
- Cohort effects
- Learning styles
- Conversation styles
- Insight
- Interests
- Political affiliation

Core Element 4: Financial

Money affects everyone's daily life. Because of this, everyone has an opinion about it, and how to spend it. Do you think of money as fun, or as something sacred which should only be saved? A person's lifestyle is most often dictated by his or her type of financial philosophy, so it is important to find a person who shares your ideas about money. Aspects of financial style are:

- Lifestyle
- Ideas about money
- Spending style
- Savings
- Investments
- Opinions about debt
- Purchases
- Retirement
- Goals

Core Element 5: Spiritual

Spirituality isn't necessarily one's religious orientation. Rather, it is someone's basic belief system about life in general. It is the sense of self people feel when they wake up in the morning, and it drives them all day long. It is their reason for living. Spirituality includes beliefs about:

- Values
- Thoughts of life
- Ethics
- Religion
- Importance of religion
- Definition of spirituality
- Family values
- Purpose of life
- Optimism
- Negativism
- Conversation
- Acceptance of others
- Integrity
- Trustworthiness
- Honesty
- Responsibility
- Societal values

Using the Core Elements to Make a Match

Whenever you are interested in a man, it is important to know his views on each of the five components. The more areas of comparability, the stronger the foundation of the relationship will be. People can have differences, but it adds strain to a relationship.

Here is a graph comparing Mark's five core elements (the Xs) with Ashley's (the Os). It is very clear to see how differently each views the individual aspects of themselves. To have a healthy relationship, each person needs to match closely, not necessarily exactly, on the same scale as the other. For example, a very big difference is apparent between Ashley's "1" on the importance of sexual issues in her life compared to Mark's "5" on the same scale. Very early in the relationship they would experience conflict in the sexual aspect of their lives because they each view sex differently. Also, their intellectual scale has a three-point discrepancy, which would also create conflict for the couple. The other three areas, spirituality, emotional, and financial, were ranked closely, which means they have complementary views on the three areas.

	Emotional	Sexual	Intellectual	Financial	Spiritual
5		X	X		
4					XO
3	O				
2	X		O	X	
1		O		O	

Another example is the relationship between Ellen and Frank. In the newness of their relationship, all five aspects appeared to match up beautifully. Emotionally they got along like two high-spirited children out playing for the day. They drove around in his convertible rummaging through thrift shops in search of their favorite childhood record albums, walking along the beach, having lunch at sidewalk cafes, or getting tipsy in the country while wine tasting. In the evenings they put on their proper adult clothing and drove to parties in his Rolls Royce, interacting on the same intellectual level and discussing abstract concepts with interesting people. Financially, they both liked to spend money and enjoyed weekend excursions to new areas or throwing great parties. Religion played no part in either of their lives; however, they were both highly spiritual and loved to discuss insights, theories, and ideas while they sat enjoying each other for hours. The problems eventually arose in the sexual category. Ellen was never highly attracted to Frank in a sexual way but enjoyed his sexual nature. His sexual tastes grew more intense and aberrant for her to take part in. This discrepancy eventually led to the downfall of a once perfect relationship.

The example of Ellen and Frank shows the importance of how just one area of great difference can create severe problems for a couple. It is important that you really get to know the person you are dating to see whether the relationship has longevity written in it.

Who Is the Man Who *Can* Commit?

Some qualities are common to all Mr. Rights. First, his life is in order, he's employed, stable, reliable, and has been out of a relationship long enough to be over the rebound period (one and one-half years). He is a man who feels satisfied with every aspect of life except for one. He has no one to share it with. This is the man that everyone likes to fix up because he is such a good catch. Emotionally he's healthy and doesn't carry old baggage.

Men who can commit won't be found in a bar or a singles hangout. These are the men who stay home on Saturday nights because they have lost interest in the dating meat market scene. They avoid the singles scene, so don't go there looking for someone. As a matter of fact, only three types of men frequent the bars, singles parties, and singles events: noncommitters, men on the rebound, and married men looking for an innocent victim to lie to.

Another fact about men who can commit is that they are more likely to join the upper-scale dating services to find a mate. They are serious about finding a partner and are willing to pay for someone to do the searching that they don't have the time or energy for.

Screening for the Man
Who Can Commit

Congratulations! You're heading in the right direction when a number of the points listed here show up in a relationship. Check the ones that apply to your situation.

1. He is on a consistent, assertive campaign to find "the woman of his dreams."
2. He is a good listener and always interested in whatever you have to say.
3. He is readily available when you need him.
4. He is concerned about others and willing to help.
5. He's punctual and dependable.
6. His home needs a woman's touch.
7. He makes good eye contact.
8. He's more interested in feelings rather than trying to impress you with material things.
9. His gifts are from the heart, personalized to you, and show thoughtfulness.
10. He makes love—he doesn't just have sex.
11. He's happy to be with you and will parade you around his friends and family.
12. He takes you to public places; he doesn't hide you.
13. He holds hands with you in public.
14. After sex, he spends the night.
15. He cuddles with you.
16. He's respectful of your goals and supports you all the way.
17. He's patient with you.
18. He has firm boundaries and doesn't let people take advantage of him.

———

Dear Diary . . .

It's Thursday night and the charity calls begin. Beverly was first to call, sure I would want to go out with her friend the investment banker. Been there, done that. Next!

Jill called next with her offering. Claiming to have found my soul mate, "Mr. Attorney." I've tasted. I've spit out. Next!

Tina offered twins, one a doctor, one a rocker. Narcissism and drugs? No thanks. Pass. Next!

It's Saturday night and I have a little problem. Friday night blues led to Saturday night woes, three of them all due at seven.

Ring. Ring. Oh, no, the time has come, I have to decide— only one can be chosen. "Hello." Passive relief. It's only my waitress friend. "Your favorite kind of man is here: 'Mr. CEO.'"

Dashing out, I tape a note to the door—three men, three words: "I'll explain later."

———

7

How a Man's Profession and Birth Order Affect You

People choose jobs that complement their personality type. For instance, a man who is aggressive will go into sales. A man who is caring and gentle will go into the human service field. Someone ambitious will work his way to the top of his profession and be the boss. Do you know what kind of man, based on his job title, is best for you? Most women don't. This is because most women go through life without a search plan, just accepting men who come their way as opposed to looking for a specific type of man.

It's very easy to learn what type of profession is most complementary to yours. All you have to do is write out which personality characteristics you find desirable. Take a minute right now and list the top five qualities you find attractive in a man:

1. _____

2. _____

3. _____

4. _____

5. _____

When I asked Stephanie to make a list of the characteristics she wanted, she came up with the following:

1. Outgoing

2. Gregarious

3. Outdoor type

4. Intelligent

5. Logical thinkers

Based on her list, what kind of job would you think fit these characteristics? How about firemen, salesmen, and marketing men? Sure they do. However, Stephanie's ignorance of stereotypes limited her ability to find a compatible partner. Stephanie complained that her boyfriends were always boring. It made a lot of sense when she explained that she worked in an aerospace company and dated the engineers who worked there. Stephanie fell victim to her environment and dated the engineers for two reasons: it was convenient and easy to find a date where she worked, and she was attracted to their logical thinking and intelligence. Engineers, if you don't already know, are stereotypically introverted, shy, intelligent, and logical thinkers. As for spontaneous, outgoing, and exciting, they are not. Stephanie needed a man with all five of her qualities, not only two, to be happy.

Stephanie found a perfect match for her when she discovered men in the marketing field. They were outgoing, gregarious, intelligent, logical thinkers, and some even liked the outdoors. As a bonus, she loved their creative thinking.

Many women are like Stephanie and date men who have only some of the qualities they are looking for. You don't have to compromise; you only have to discover what qualities you want in a man. The next step is to figure out which profession attracts that type of man. Don't worry if you don't think this way now, because this chapter will teach you how.

What Kind of Job, Man, and Woman Go Together?

Little girls grow up idealizing the man they will marry. Inevitably, they dream of doctors and lawyers. There is one problem with this. Not all women's temperaments are compatible with those personality types. The goal of this chapter is to help you identify your "type" of man according to the type of job he has.

Stereotypes

It is not politically correct to judge someone on a stereotype, but it serves a purpose here, so we'll do it anyway! Stereotypes make it possible for women to know, beforehand, the general characteristics a man will have before she even meets him. Stereotypes also make it possible for a woman to focus on a certain "type" of man she will search for as a partner, which eliminates wasted hours aimlessly looking for a man. Instead, if she knows what kind of job the man has, she can concentrate her search in that field only. That creates a higher probability that she will find a compatible partner.

Birth Order and Job Type

Birth order is another tool you can use to categorize a man's personality when you first meet him. For many reasons, a man's personality is somewhat determined by the placement he was born into. Each birth in a family changes the structure and affects everyone involved. These differences create an environment in which each child is treated in a unique way and results in each person developing a distinct identity and interaction pattern. This is the beginning of how one aspect of someone's personality is developed. Personalities don't change much as a person ages, so they tend to react to many of the events in their life the same way they reacted to them in their family of origin. Murray Bowen, a family systems therapist, believes that "n single piece of data is more important than knowing the sibl; position of people." When searching for a partner, it is he]

to use all the tools you can to screen for the best possible partner you can find.

Characteristics of a Man's Birth Order

1. The Oldest Child

Did you know that many very successful people are
the oldest or only children in a family? This is because
they grew up experiencing high expectations from parents, and interact from an early age in an adult world.
They develop a work ethic early in childhood, instead of
a frolicking sense of self. This impacts the core of who
they develop into as adults. Below are additional characteristics of what types of people oldest and only children
often become:

- Impatient and demanding with people
- Have good verbal skills
- Have good social skills
- Have good learning techniques
- High achievers
- Educated
- Responsible
- Protective of others
- Nurturing
- Responsible
- Perfectionist
- Worriers
- Don't like to disappoint people
- Have trouble accepting mistakes by others
- Conform to what is expected of them
- Pessimistic
- Compulsive and/or obsessive/compulsive
- Hard workers
- Associate fun with immaturity
- Need a lot of admiration and respect from others
- Appear arrogant

- Have difficulty accepting criticism, even the constructive kind
- Have a hard time admitting they are wrong
- Tend to overcommit themselves
- Don't know how to say no
- Find it difficult to ask for help
- Express anger verbally

2. **Middle Children**

   These children struggle the most in families. They learn to fight hard in order to stand out from the prized oldest child and the adorable baby of the family. Their identity is developed out of the energy they put into getting noticed. As adults, they are a little more aggressive, dramatic, and have more "character" than most other birth orders. Read on to learn more about their natures. Middle children often:

- Feel overlooked or left out
- Feel somewhat unwanted
- Compete for attention
- Are competitive in nature
- Have a moody nature
- Feel that life is unfair
- Are low achievers
- Are sensitive
- Good negotiators
- Find it easy to ask for help
- Prefer to be with others
- Are peacemakers
- Sometimes appear inconsistent and prone to waffle
- Try to live in harmony
- Maintain high family involvement as a mediator
- Have identity problems and problems with self-esteem
- Are good listeners
- Are creative thinkers
- Are anxious
- Do things to get attention

- May be dramatic or histrionic
- Are critical of self
- Give up easily
- Argue easily but make up quickly
- Are less competitive than other birth orders
- Have low expectations for self
- Make friends easily
- Are flexible
- Don't accept praise well
- Stay in destructive relationships longer

3. **Youngest Children**

   Many times the youngest in the family lives a carefree life in which he or she can do no wrong. Youngest children live in a world of less restriction and fewer guidelines than middle or older children. They are used to getting their own way, or having others step in and do things for them. They are spoiled and wouldn't want life any other way. As adults, they grow up with the same sense of entitlement, and expect to maintain that role with everyone they come in contact with. The following characteristics describe them:

   - Always the baby in the family
   - Used to being babied
   - Expect others to do things for them
   - Like a lot of attention and praise
   - Expect to be pampered
   - Cope well in messy environments
   - Don't get upset easily
   - Not anxious
   - Difficult to make them angry
   - Live a life of indulgences
   - Expect nice things
   - Have a sense of entitlement
   - Optimistic about life
   - Manipulators
   - Lead undisciplined lives

- Spontaneous
- Procrastinators
- Find order and structure difficult
- Dependent personalities
- Narcissistic

4. Only Children

These children are the most indulged, spoiled with praise, material goods, and attention. They usually have a strong sense of self because of their many accomplishments. The drawback is that stress typically accompanies the members of this birth placement because they try to please everyone who is important to them. As adults, they have the following characteristics:

- Perfectionistic
- Mature
- Serious
- Hard on self
- Good social skills
- Well-developed verbal skills
- High achievers
- Poor at sharing
- Need a lot of space and quiet time
- Creative thinkers
- Not comfortable around children
- Have a lot of insight
- Intuitive
- Afraid of criticism
- Afraid of failure
- Good imagination
- Less playful
- Live structured lives
- Conform to rules
- Traditional
- Have a broad range of interests
- Not talkative

- Parents' role in their lives very important
- "Mama's boy"
- Selfish
- Problem solver
- Spoiled
- Like to have their own way
- Expect others to baby them
- Not good at apologizing

Don't expect all men you meet to have every characteristic of his birth order category. If the man is the baby of his family, for instance, he should have many of the items listed. But remember, no two men are exactly alike because each experiences different family settings and experiences.

You will find that many of the characteristics cited for birth order are the same characteristics you will find in the various job categories. This is because jobs attract certain types of people with certain personality types. Many attorneys are either older children or middle children because they have the personality skills to get the job done. You will also find many only children and oldest children in highly successful jobs because their characteristics as well match what is required for their chosen profession. Art usually attracts middle children and the babies of families because of a need for attention or the unstructured lifestyle. The reasons vary for why people go into their chosen field, but the point is that their paths occur because of the comfort they feel in that area.

Types of Men

Let's get back to the topic of dating and analyzing the men you date. Ask yourself, "Do the men I date usually fall into the same job category each time? If so, what is it? And what about those men typically attracts me to them?" List the characteristics in a notebook to refer to later. When describing the man's characteristics, remember to focus on the internal aspects of the man rather than the physical. You will soon discover which job category draws men with the appealing characteristics you are after.

On the next few pages, you will find popular job categories in which men work. I interviewed twenty men from each job listed. From that I developed categories of their personality characteristics, based on how they described themselves.

Directions
1. Place a check next to every characteristic that you find attractive.

2. Don't mark the characteristic if you aren't sure whether it is appealing to you.

3. When you finish, one category should have more check marks in it than the others. That will be your first step in identifying your type of man.

White-Collar/Professional Jobs

Marketing, Lawyer, Businessman, Doctor
Aggressive

Driven

Selfish

Demanding

Narcissistic

Captivating

Disciplined lifestyle

Engaging

Dominates conversation with his interests

Interesting

Stimulating

Requires a lot of attention

Enjoys talking about his own accomplishments

Condescending

Confident

Likes to talk in-depth about ideas and plans

Has a strong need for respect
Requires a lot of mental stimulation
Impatient with slowness from a partner
Tends to be a perfectionist
Experiences life through thoughts more than feelings
Prefers an adult world, not a child's world
Short-tempered or emotionally distant
High expectations for self as well as others
Treats children as adults
Intelligent, well-educated
Deep thinker
Exceedingly independent
Less importance for religion
Argumentative
Work is his priority

Technician, Professor, Engineer

Introverted
Passive
Tendency toward passive-aggressiveness
Shy
Not in touch with his feelings
Logical
Leads a quiet life
Factual
Intelligent
Enjoys structured activities
Lives vicariously through reading
Educated
Perfectionist

Worries silently

Holds emotions in

Conforms to what is expected of him

Hard worker

People pleaser

Conforms to society

Rarely shows anger

Responsible

Poor social skills

Not comfortable being spontaneous

Serious

Analytical

Enjoys time alone

Hard on self

Family man

Not talkative

Problem solver

Not good at apologizing

Blue-Collar Workers

Police Officer, Cashier, Construction Worker

Family oriented

Good basic values

Religious

Hardworking

Cooperative

Follower

Team player

Devotion to children first, then mate

Dependable

Loyal

Traditional

High school education at most

Expects mate to take care of him

Beer drinker

Leads separate life from mate

Believes in having "boys' night out"

Salespeople

General Salesman, Stockbroker, Car Salesman

Charismatic

Pushy

Persistent

Smooth talker

Superficial

Talented at small talk

Good sense of humor

Gregarious

Extroverted

Selfish

Confident

Wanderer

Manipulative

Independent

Moody

Self-esteem issues

Pessimistic about life

Cynical

Low achiever

Competitive

Anxious

Sensitive but may not show it

Critical of self

Low expectations of self

Creative Men

Musician, Artist, Writer

Passionate

Unstructured

Unreliable

Spiritual

Freespirited

Nonconformist

Independent thinker

Loner

Creative

Right-brained thinker

Spontaneous

Doesn't like pressure

Moody

Temperamental

Self-centered

Traditional Jobs

Teacher, Social Worker

Traditional values

Family oriented

Compassionate

Nurturing

Sensitive to the needs of others

Tendency to worry easily

Introverted

Religious

Supportive

Family man

Responsible

Even tempered

Honors commitments

Worries but tries to hide it

Good negotiator

Humble

Dear Diary . . .

Just the thought of getting ready for my date tonight exhausts me. Pulling out my favorite red dress from the closet. The tag reads a size 4. My contrary image of a size 6 is seen in the full-length mirror. I believe the tag's number. No problem. It's all about manipulation, sculpting, camouflage, and denial. Basically, hiding and lying.

Out of the shower. I go to work on resculpting my body. Thigh cream, control top pantyhose, and the Wonderbra.

Across the room I see my competition—the size 4 dress. My thoughts bounce back and forth between insecurity and confidence as I stride toward the red material. Dropping my size 10 robe, I stand there ready to challenge my size. Slipping my body through the openings, sliding the dress down, the challenge of the zipper still awaits. Calling for help, my roommate decides the final score as she takes on the challenge of zipping me in. She calls out, making the final decision, "You look great. Size 4 and all." I knew I could do it!

8

How to Dress to Attract Men

Many women forget the importance of a first impression. In the previous chapter, you discovered what kind of job a man will take based on his personality characteristics. Now you will learn how to dress to attract that particular type of man.

Women know the importance clothing can make on others. A woman will wear a sexy dress to arouse a date's interest. She will wear a blazer to cover her sexuality. She will wear a suit to appear professional. Most women have learned "how to dress for success," but not many give thought to the kind of men they attract based on what they wear.

Dressing to Attract Men with Money

When it comes to fashion, wealthy men seem to like certain looks on women.

1. *A confident look.* In a business situation, a blue or beige suit with a contrasting blouse is a good choice. A good role model for this style of dressing is Princess Diana.

2. *A sporty look.* The key here is to wear the appropriate looks for each activity you do. When playing tennis, wear a tennis outfit. When boating, wear sailing clothing. To get an

idea of this type of dressing, turn on the sports channels and see how the professionals dress. You can also look through clothing catalogues to see how they coordinate the individual pieces.

3. *An evening/cocktail/elegant look.* For parties and evening wear, an evening dress is best. Dresses can be very simple or tastefully flashy. Quality is what counts, and accessories are important. You will find these dresses in the dressy dress section of any department store.

4. *A feminine look.* For men who like the feminine look, they like to see women in soft, silky dresses and frilly skirts and lace, all made of expensive materials.

5. *The exotic look.* To attain this look, find unique pieces of clothing that make a statement. Women in the nighttime drama shows usually dress this way, especially shows that center around wealthy families. Many women on soap operas also dress in this style.

The most important point about attracting a man of wealth is to dress in the right clothing for each activity or event. An exotic look, for example, at a sporting event would not work. Common places to purchase the items are at high-priced stores (e.g., Nordstrom's). For those on a budget, you can still dress the part by shopping at upscale secondhand stores and discount designer stores (e.g., Nordstrom's Rack).

Dressing to Attract Professional Men

Marketing Men, Lawyers, Businessmen

These men like women who dress the way they do, in suits and expensive clothes. The easiest way to get a feel for this type of clothing is to look through popular women's magazines. These are clothes that can go from a business meeting to an evening out. Like men of wealth, these men believe in wearing different outfits for different occasions such as golf clothing for playing golf and tennis clothing for a game of tennis.

Technicians, Professors, Engineers

This professional category of men is very particular. They like women who wear just the right things, shapes, and colors, presenting a very complete picture. Be careful not to wear items of clothing that clash. These men like lines and solids. Scientists and engineers do not like high fashion. The place to shop is department stores.

Dressing to Attract "Working Men"

Police Officers, Cashiers, Construction Workers

The men in this category tend to dress in middle-class clothing, but they like their women to look good. These men like women who wear a seductive or sexy look. They like to see flesh and curves. Tight jeans on a woman are very attractive to these men. They aren't interested in styles or color but how sexy the woman looks.

General Salesmen, Stockbrokers, Car Salesmen

These men prefer a woman who is versatile in her dress. They like women who can wear a suit during the day and jeans at night. After work hours they like to take their suits off and spend time in comfortable clothes like the women they spend time with. The style of dress for this woman is not high fashion or conservative; it is casual and down-to-earth. To find this type of clothing, you can shop in stores like Miller's Outpost, Ross, or any reasonably priced women's store at a mall.

Musicians, Artists, Writers

These men are attracted to women whose clothing reflect that they have artistic ability. Using color well is important here, but high fashion is not. Being quite presentable is the key with these men. The places to shop for clothes in this category are secondhand stores or artistic type of stores.

Depending on the type of man you want to attract, you will
have to dress according to what he finds attractive. If you don't,
then he is more likely to miss seeing you when he is out in
public. For the most part, men like women who look like they
do. So do your homework and keep your eye on women who
date the type of men you want to date. Let them be your fashion advisers from afar to teach you the way to dress to attract
the man you want.

———————

Dear Diary . . .
   *While boarding a plane to visit a potential lover in Hawaii,
I saw him. David. Confident and intense. Feeling like a cat,
I became curious. Stalking him, I moved in. My whiskers
ruffled. A plaything. A new trophy for my collection. An air-
plane catch. What a rare find. He came my way. Electricity
danced in the air. Closer. Closer. Caught! Purring began as
our conversation approached intimacy. We went our ways.
Him for a vacation. Me to another man. So dramatic. So
much fun. Confident he'll call. They always do!*

———————

9

Where to Find a Man

Most women are going to be aware of what I'm about to discuss—where to find your ideal man. However, most women don't think about where the men are. Consider this: what is it that most men do during their workdays? That's right, they work. So, if you want to find a man, go to his workplace. Or go near his workplace. That's why it's so important for you to figure out what kind of man you like and what kind of job he has.

Let's say that you want a man in retail. Where do you go to find one? You go shopping at the mall. If you want an attorney, where do you go? You go to his office, a law library, or you go to the courthouse. You go where these men spend their time. If you want a bartender, all of a sudden you realize you need a drink, so you head to a bar. That's how you do it. You go to his workplace.

Bridget always fantasized about having a firefighter for a boyfriend, but she didn't know how to meet one unless she was to call 911 to report a fire. That approach would guarantee that she would meet them; however, it would make a lot of people very angry. One day she got lost in an unfamiliar town and decided to stop at a firehouse to ask for directions. For the next month, she drove around town, stopping at different firehouses

ostensibly to ask for directions. She got lucky and met a wonderful fireman named Matt.

The Dr. Romance Formula for Finding Him

This formula consists of looking for men during daytime
hours, during the week only. This approach cuts out the
evening and weekend searching. The men you meet during the
day will be much more open to having a conversation with you
than they would at a bar while they struggle to think of "come-
on" lines. Men feel more at ease because they don't feel like it's
a pickup time or they're at a meat market. So, you both feel
much more comfortable, and a relationship is more likely to
happen.

What You Need to Know Before You Begin

Before you start your search to find Mr. Right, you need to
know the following things about a man:

1. What type of man are you attracted to physically and
   emotionally?
2. What type of job do you want the man to have?
3. What relationship patterns would you like to avoid?

After answering these questions, you should be able to have
a good idea of what type of man you want. Now I want you
to turn to Chapter 11, "Use the Yellow Pages!" to help you
narrow your search and give you exact addresses of where the
men are.

Other Guides for Finding a Man

Organizations

Men like to join associations and clubs related to their hobbies
and jobs. At the reference desk in all libraries, you will find a
listing of every organization in existence. Librarians love to help

you locate things, so don't hesitate to ask for their assistance. Men who need to work on presentation skills join organizations for public speaking such as Toast Masters International. Men interested in the arts join performing arts organizations. The list is endless, and your opportunities are great.

The Newspaper

An important resource manual for women who are looking for men is the newspaper. The newspaper gives a lot of information about what is going on in the community. From now on, look at the newspaper differently. Keeping your "type" of man in mind, ask yourself what section of the newspaper would your ideal man read? If he is a businessman, he will read the business section. If he is a "manly man," he will read the sports section.

While reading these sections, scan the advertisements. See what activities are being advertised for him. Advertisers market their ads because they know the people who read those sections are more likely to put their dollars toward their products. For example, men in sales will be attracted to advertisements for motivational seminars. Single fathers who are family men will read the community calendar section and respond to ads such as "Disney on Ice" or "Children's Museum."

Most women complain about not knowing where the men are. This excuse will no longer work for you because the newspaper advertisements tell you where he spends his free time. Did you hear that? Now you know where he will be . . . just waiting for you to arrive so that he can meet you.

How It Works   Let's say you want a man who's interested in outdoor activities. What you do is turn to the appropriate newspaper section, perhaps the sports pages. Listed there weekly are all the sporting activities and clubs in the area. There will be a list of aerobics classes, archery classes, baseball, tennis, handball, hiking, golf, and every sport imaginable. All you do is pick a sport that you enjoy and show up at the scheduled time and place. He'll have no idea you are there to meet someone just like him.

Keep in mind that men and women are creatures of habit. This means that if you go to two meetings, you are likely to meet all of the regular members. Don't waste your time going week after week, hoping a new man will show up. If you aren't attracted to any of them, move on to a new group to check out its members. Eventually you will find a group that has a member you like.

Another example: if you want a doctor, look in the community section of the newspaper. There you will find health fairs that will be filled with caring doctors for you to meet. If you are interested in meeting a plastic surgeon, they advertise seminars all the time.

Worksheet for Finding a Man Through the Newspaper   These questions are intended to help you develop a road map to follow that will help you find your man:

1. What kind of man would you like to meet?

   _____

   _____

2. What kinds of interests would you like for him to have?

   _____

   _____

3. What section of the newspaper would he be likely to read?

   _____

   _____

4. What kinds of activities are listed in the sections he is likely to read?

   _____

   _____

5. Write down the information from the ads that you find in
   the sections of the newspaper he is likely to read.

   _____

   _____

   _____

Dear Diary . . .

  *Filled with enthusiasm, ready for the hunt, and looking
good. I'm ready for a generous boyfriend. Here I stand before
my mirror, decorated with tokens from past loves. The Tiffany
watch from Lee. The gold bracelet from Fred. And the Chanel
suit from David. New Age "Collect-um," I think it's called.
What a way to be outfitted. However, I still need shoes and a
bag to match. Off to retrieve these items. I'm meeting Steve
for lunch . . . at the mall. Need I say more?*

   _____

10

How to Get It Together for a Date

Many women dread two aspects of dating someone new. First is being asked, "Where would you like to go?" It is just as difficult for a woman to come up with ideas as it is for a man. The first thing that pops into your head is the predictable "Dinner." Okay, dinner, then what? Second, many women are uncomfortable about what to talk about on a date.

The five-minute Sunday homework habit puts an end to what to do and awkward silences. By the end of this chapter, those hindrances will never happen to you again. The following pages are full of suggestions that will be handy when a man calls you for a date and asks that dreaded question.

Materials Needed:
Newspaper, Scissors, and Post-It Notes

These are the only things you need to make this project effective. As for the newspaper, you will only need three sections of it: the entertainment section; the front page; and the section about home, family, and community. Feel free to use more of the paper if you have the time. From the three sections you will be able to find many ideas for dates and conversation topics.

How to Use This Chapter

The first thing you need to do is get a notebook for this section. On the next few pages you will find various subject headings. In your notebook, label one page for each subject: Restaurants, Favorite Movies, Outdoor Activities, and Small-Talk Enrichers. Each section will direct you. For now, all you need to know is that you will be asked to cut out various things related to each topic and tape it on the appropriate page. You may find that some articles are too large to use. In that case, it is best to write the information down on a Post-It note and stick it on the page. Avoid writing directly on the blank page because you will periodically need to take away and add new ideas to the pages.

When you are finished with this chapter, you can forget experiencing panic attracks as a result of the dreaded question mentioned earlier. All you will have to do is say, "Well, let me think. . . ." As he waits for you to come up with an idea, you can reach for your notebook, open to the appropriate page, and say confidently, "I know about a great mystery dinner train ride." What comfort! So go ahead, spend the next five minutes finding things you enjoy.

Restaurants

Restaurants are listed in the entertainment section of the newspaper. The listings typically give you the price range, from inexpensive to very expensive with a couple of categories in between. Other than the address and phone number, the restaurants are listed in categories of food types. Everyone likes to eat, so you can be assured he'll appreciate the suggestion. In your notebook, tape the restaurants that you would like to try. Make sure that you have their phone numbers and addresses. Since you don't know much about the man and his finances on a first date, it is always a good idea to suggest a couple of different places and let him decide. For instance, suggesting a Mexican restaurant lets the man know that it is inexpensive as opposed to a higher-priced French restaurant.

Rules About Restaurants

1. If you are not sure about what to suggest, you can't go wrong with a moderately priced restaurant. This way you don't come across as having cheap taste, and you don't look like a gold digger. It's up to you, though. I know women who will only go to the finest restaurants and won't date men who don't have the money to afford them. Then again, I know of other women who feel too guilty to let men pay for dinner, and they insist on making dinner for them.

2. Never suggest using a coupon on a first date. It sets the man's standards of you very low. Some women try to please men from the very minute they meet them. Genie Polo Sayles, an expert on how to marry the rich, once said, "A man shows how much he values you by how much money he invests in you." I agree with this: men do put money toward what they value, including women.

3. Never suggest to pay for your half of the dinner. If a man asks you to dinner, he knows that he is going to be paying. Some women believe that they should pay for dinner if they ask a man out. This is wrong. A man should always pay for dinner regardless of who asks. Romance is about being courted; let him pay to court you. Men love to pay—it makes them feel like they are making an investment in you. If a man ever asks you to pay, simply decline. Take him on a picnic or make dinner for him if you feel you owe him something, but never pay for your dinner.

4. Try to choose restaurants that offer entertainment, such as a murder mystery or live music. It makes silent gaps easier to handle and gives your dinner an obvious point of conversation.

5. Choose a restaurant near a place where the two of you can walk after dinner. Places by the beach, lakes, or parks are great.

6. Don't talk about other men on a date; men hate it! I mention this because an overwhelming amount of men have told me that women do this all the time on dates.

Favorite Movies

Open up your Sunday newspaper. Look for movies that you would like to see. I don't recommend going to a movie early on in the dating process. Dating should be used as qualifying time. The only way you can learn about a man is by talking with him. Why should you waste your time dating someone who isn't going to work out in the end? Go ahead and still have fun on your dates, but your goal is to discover who the man is to see whether he falls into your "Mr. Wrong" pattern. If your pattern isn't bad, then go ahead, have fun, do whatever you want—just enjoy yourself.

Survey Results About Men and Movies

If you do decide to go to a movie on a first, second, or third date, keep in mind the following results from a study I conducted about dating. The study included 50 questions regarding dating relationships between men and women. The participants were 25 men and 25 women ranging in age from 25 to 60.

- Out of 20 activities listed that people typically do on dates, movies ranked as the most likely type of date to be cancelled. These results were ranked the same for both men and women.
- The type of date least canceled were dates requiring the most amount of preparation and money.
- Men felt more uncomfortable compared to women when watching highly sexually explicit movies.
- Men were more likely to have sex after watching a violent movie as opposed to comedy, romantic, or even sexually explicit movie.
- Men preferred watching comedies on a first movie date.
- Men reported feeling uncomfortable with intimacy in the movie theater compared to women. The ranking order is listed here, from most to least uncomfortable. The preferred

behavior, surprisingly, was not touching at all during the movie. The most common reason for this answer was because it was too hard to get comfortable in the seats to enjoy the intimacy. The second most common reason to the answer was due to embarrassment of public displays of affection.

1. Kissing
2. Having a woman put her arm around a man's shoulder
3. Snuggling
4. Caressing
5. Arm around woman's shoulder
6. Hand holding

Outdoor Activities

Outdoor activities can include so many things: sporting events, lectures, museums, cruises, or anything that gets you out of a restaurant or movie theater. For this section, you need to use either the entertainment or sports section of the newspaper. Search through the sections carefully to find things you would enjoy doing. When it comes time to suggest a date activity, you don't want to mention something you would dread doing just because you think your date would have fun.

Small-Talk Enrichers

Everyone shudders when there is a lull in the conversation on a first date. That's why this page is handy. Flip through the newspaper and cut out conversation topics such as current events, political topics, Ann Landers questions, popular books, and whatever else you think would fill a pregnant pause. Jot down one or two points from interesting articles on a Post-It note. If you are the type of woman who gets very nervous, it would be a good idea to review your notes before your date. An even better idea would be to practice your lines by role-playing with yourself. All you do is sit at your kitchen table and pretend to be having a conversation with your date. This kind of practice will make uncomfortable situations much easier to get through.

Suggestions from Men for First Dates

Men get tired of having to be the one who decides what to do on a date. Men are always impressed by a woman who knows what she likes and isn't afraid to suggest it.

In my interviews, a few points surfaced with most men regarding dating. First, they prefer dates that involve an activity (music, dinner show, rollerblading, listening to music, etc.) to distract from being caught with nothing to say. Second, men enjoy first dates more when the date is down-to-earth rather than too fancy or formal. Another common point the men made was about getting nervous on dates. They worry about making a good impression and saying the right things, and they become uncomfortable when they feel like they have to perform (ordering the right kind of wine and such).

Many women have the impression that men are only interested in having sex and don't care for a friendship. This is wrong—the men responded in just the opposite way. They said that having a friendship is very important and sex is just a bonus, but not the number one goal for dating.

The suggestions here are ideas for women to offer on a date, all of which came from men. They are in no particular order, so pick one or make up your own.

Great Ideas for the First Few Dates

- Sports-related activities: tennis, bowling, rollerblading, bike riding, hiking along the beach, ice skating, and so on. Don't forget to stop for lunch along the way.
- Sunday champagne brunch
- Miniature golfing
- Amusement park
- Wine tasting

- A train ride that includes a lunch or dinner
- Jazz club
- Coffeehouse with entertainment
- Double date
- Art gallery or museum
- Daytime boat adventure such as a day cruise. Avoid evening cruises because they are too romantic for dates early on in a relationship.
- A sporting event you both like
- Plays and musicals
- Seminars you both have an interest in
- Afternoon scenic drive
- A walk around a lake, with a picnic

Places to Avoid on the First Few Dates

Some things should be avoided on a first date, because they encourage artificial closeness in a romantic setting. Sometimes, women are too trusting and put themselves in a position of risk by assuming the man is "good." In today's world, it's always better to play it safe. Men know this too, which is why many of them understand when a woman declines a man's offer to pick her up for a date, saying she'll meet him instead.

- Movies—They don't allow for any interaction.
- Too much seclusion, such as hiking in the mountains—It's too trusting.
- A bar—It's too distracting and filled with lots of singles on the prowl.
- A friend's party or wedding—This makes people assume that the two of you are a couple.
- A weekend getaway—Even with separate rooms, it can be a long weekend if you decide you aren't interested in the man after all. It is easy to fake your way through an evening, but not a weekend.
- Dancing—Wait a few dates before you sweat with him.
- Dinner at your house or his—It's too intimate.

- Watching a video at home—It communicates to the man that you are not worth more.

Dating creates a lot of emotions for a woman, from excitement, to disappointment, to boredom, to anger. No one can predict how a date will turn out, but everyone hopes for the best. Dating should be fun. With the help of this chapter, you will have guidelines to help you enjoy a sometimes nerve-racking endeavor.

Dear Diary . . .

Flipping through the phone book, I'm after a new boyfriend. Lust at first sight. There, before my eyes, Dr. Pain. An endodontist. Suddenly, my tooth begins to ache. A phone call had me lying beneath him as he stared into my mouth. "The tooth is fine," he stated, kissing my cheek provocatively. Somewhat unethical, but I didn't mind one bit. Chemistry bubbled, and a relationship developed. I shouldn't kiss and tell, but I can say, the process has not been like pulling teeth.

11

Use the Yellow Pages!

This section will be a big help when you work on Chapter 9, "Where to Find a Man," where you discovered that the place to find a man is at his workplace. This search will be based on a particular profession that your personality type is compatible with. This chapter will give you an idea about the kinds of men there are and where they work.

Many women don't know what kind of professions they prefer their mates to have. Such information is an important screening device to tell you up front what his general characteristics are and whether they are what you are looking for.

To find this listing in your own phone book, open to the index pages. The contents page at the front of the book will refer you to the appropriate page. The different types of jobs are listed there in alphabetical order. Here is a shortened version of the typical jobs you will find:

accountants	acupuncturists	advertisers
ambulance drivers	animal trainers	appraisers
attorneys	bankruptcy consultants	bankers
bartenders	bookkeepers	builders
cabinet makers	cake decorators	carpenters
computer consultants	construction workers	contractors

dentists	divers	doctors
electricians	engineers	fire fighters
golf pros	government consultants	grocers
holistic practitioners	hypnotherapists	insurance agents
janitors	jewelers	karate instructors
librarians	loan officers	mail carriers
marines	morticians	paralegals
pawnbrokers	photographers	printers
property managers	psychologists	publicists
real estate agents	researchers	salespeople
school teachers	sports figures	surveyors
tax advisers	taxi drivers	travel agents
veterinarians	watchmakers	window cleaners
writers	X-ray technicians	zookeepers

The Phone Book: Find a Face You Like

After perusing your phone index, you should flip to the reference page, which will list many companies under that job category. More important, you will be able to see whether you can find any of the businesses near your home or work. Later in this book, you will use your phone book as a mate-finding guide to locate ideal men for you.

Pick a Man Who Appeals to You

My research revealed something surprising. I discovered that more than half of the people who use their photograph in their advertisements are single. So, if you find your type of profession and see a man's picture that you are attracted to, you have a 55 percent chance that he is single. (This research was conducted in Orange County, California, using the phone books for north, central, and south Orange County areas. The rates of single people who advertise with their photographs may vary in different areas.)

How to Find Out Whether He's Married

Flip through the yellow pages, page by page, looking for pictures of men you find attractive. If you see a man you like, you need to find out whether he's single. All you do is call the ad and use the following script with the person who answers the phone:

[Ring, ring]

Other end: "Hello, you've reached ___ Company."

You: "Hello. My friend gave me this number, but I'm not sure I have the right company. Is this the Joe Smith whose wife recently had twins? She said he was great and that I should call and set up an appointment" (or whatever is appropriate to the profession).

Other end, hopefully you'll hear: "No, Joe is not even married."

Julie, from one of my seminars, tried this approach and was very lucky. Knowing nothing about law, she was intrigued by an attorney's picture advertising his practice. The ad mentioned monthly informative meetings. She had a great excuse to call: she needed to register for the next meeting. She was caught off guard when "Mr. Attorney" himself answered the phone. She regained composure and inquired about the meeting. She got brave and asked him questions about his legal background since she wanted to know more about him. On the day of the meeting she arrived early to introduce herself. Luck was on her side when no one showed for the meeting. This led to them having an intimate meeting in the hotel restaurant.

Before you call an ad, keep in mind that the company receives many calls every day, so don't worry—the person on the other end will be unaware of your real motive.

Once you know the attractive man's marital status, you can progress from there. If he is single, you can do one of two things: you can make an appointment and request him specifically (your friend recommended him, remember?), or you can go to his work and follow the suggestions from the "Lunch Prowl" chapter. Have fun. Go get him!

Dear Diary . . .

A date for John's party? Having no idea where to find him, I begin the deliberateness of a plan. I need a man with depth. Monday—bookstore. I need an educated man. Tuesday— library. I need a man with a great body. Wednesday—the gym. I need a great conversationalist. Thursday—coffee- house. I need a handsome man. Friday—department store fashion show. I need a man to impress my mother. Satur- day—a visit to the doctor. A phone call and an hour later the perfect date. Depth, educated, great body, great conversation- alist, handsome, and definitely someone my mother would be proud of—Craig. My date. My brother.

12

How to Keep Track of Your Men

Would you like to have a relationship with a compatible man? If your answer is yes, then you're going to have to make it happen. Ask yourself the following question: How much time do you spend right now trying to meet men on a weekly basis? Many women spend at least five hours, once a week, out with "the girls" in an attempt to meet a man. Quite honestly, that is a waste of five hours in an attempt to find something that isn't easy to find. By keeping a calendar, you will be able to allot a certain amount of time to your directed search. You will be able to fit it into what you are already doing. This method produces incredible results. In this chapter, you will find a calendar to use when planning to meet men.

How a Calendar Will Benefit You

Like most things in life, if you plan, you will save time and effort. The same thing applies to finding a man. If you are looking, you will know exactly how much time you have, where you are going, and be dressed to get the attention of the man you want. This approach gives you an advantage because you won't be caught off guard when you approach men or when they come up to you. You will secretly know you are on a mission and prepared to play the game.

How to Keep a Calendar

What you do with your calendar is schedule a time, once or twice a week, when you plan to look for a man. On that day, remember to dress similar to the type of man you want to attract.

The Dr. Romance Formula

1. Flirting is done during daytime hours only.
2. Flirting is done during the week only.
3. Schedule "prowl" or flirting times only once or twice a week.
4. Make flirting outings a solo activity to encourage men to approach you.
5. Whatever type of man you would like to find, you need to dress accordingly. For instance, if you'd like businessmen, you need to dress in business fashion. If you want a student, dress in jeans and a T-shirt.

Five-Day Calendar

The purpose of this calendar is to help you organize your search for your ideal man.

Monday	Tuesday	Wednesday	Thursday	Friday

Dear Diary . . .

*Warning: Hungry animal. Loose and on the hunt. The
sound of my alarm awakens me. What a fortuitous dream.
Feeling odd, I realize that a metamorphosis has occurred. In
the darkness of the night my mind had been invaded with
that of a fox. A sly one. Timely, I must admit. Today is my
lunch prowl, my hunting expedition. The prey, a man. Plan of
attack . . . cage his mind with an intriguing presence. Torture
him with an addiction that only I possess. And set him free
with a longing for what he needs—me.*

13

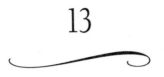

The Lunch Prowl

The only way to find a pool of different men is to look in unfamiliar places. In this chapter, you will learn precisely how to do that. The lunch prowl is simply using your lunch hour to locate men. This means that you will need to break your typical lunchtime routine and follow the techniques in this chapter. It's time to put an end to isolating yourself at work and get yourself exposed to new men.

Lunch is the best time to meet a man because most men are out looking for food between the hours of 11:30 A.M. until 1:30 P.M. Chapter 7, titled "How a Man's Profession and Birth Order Affect You," will help you learn what kind of man to look for. After reading that chapter, if you are still unsure about what kind of profession to target during lunch, then spend your lunch hours sampling the various types of professions until you develop a favorite type. Once you know your type, you will find lunch to be an easy way to meet a man because they go to predictable places—restaurants or locations near their work.

Scouting the Premises

The least suspecting time to meet a man is during the lunch hour. This is a time when the main thing on a man's mind is eating. It is a great time to catch him off guard and to catch him for yourself.

Now that you understand the meaning of lunch, you need to develop a plan of attack once you get there. Since married and single men eat together, your first step will be to make sure the men you find interesting aren't married. Review Chapter 6, "Men to Avoid," to learn the signs of married men.

The next thing to do is locate a place for you to sit that is visible yet makes you approachable if a man decides to come your way. If you are new to this, then now is the time to deal with your nervousness. Turn to Chapter 18, "How to Master Nervousness," to learn various techniques to soothe your butterflies.

Tips You Must Know About Men and Lunch

1. They go to lunch either within walking distance from their work or within 5 minutes' driving time.

2. Although men try to busy themselves with mindless activities, they would rather have a woman to talk with.

3. Women complain that men no longer make the first move. Don't hesitate to meet a man you are interested in. Keep in mind that no one cares if you want to meet another person. The only way you will meet him is if you take the initiative.

4. Single men eat at the bars in restaurants more often than at a table by themselves. So don't make the mistake of eating at a table in the dining room when you are looking for a man.

5. Men don't usually take girlfriends to lunch. So, if you see him with a woman, the occasion is probably work related.

6. Men who take early or late lunches usually eat alone, which makes it easier for you to meet them.

How to Get a Man to Talk to You: "The Lunch Prowl"

The whole goal of going on a lunch prowl is to meet men. This, unfortunately, is the most uncomfortable part about being single. To make the experience a little easier, I've listed several things that you can do to get a man to talk to you.

1. Go to lunch alone on your lunch prowl days.
2. Avoid going to "women" type of places such as diet restaurants.
3. Don't conspicuously look at every man who walks by. Be selective. Qualify men from a distance if you can to avoid catching eyes with every man who walks past you at close range. To learn how to qualify a man, turn to Chapter 16, "How to Find His Faults Before You *Know* He's Wrong."
4. Talk to people around you so you appear friendly and approachable.
5. Slow your pace down. Give men a chance to notice you.
6. Ask for instructions, directions, or whatever.
7. Ask whether you can sit at his table.
8. Ask to borrow a pen.

The last thing you need to do once you meet a man is bring the meeting to a close by using exit lines of acceptance if you want to see him again and exit lines of rejection if you don't like him. Refer to Chapters 21 and 24, respectively, on each of these subjects for ideas.

How the Prowl Works

As an example, let me tell you about Diana. She is a single mother, age 34. Diana starts her approach on Sunday evening by looking at her calendar. She schedules a lunch time, once a week, that she sets aside to look for potential mates. She pencils in "Lunch Prowl." That will be the day of the week when she will dress appropriately to attract her type of man. Therefore, the rest of the week she does not focus on the topic. That saves her a lot of time. When the "Lunch Prowl" day arrives, she gets her mind set, dresses appropriately, and focuses on her mission during the lunch hour. Diana's goal is to find a wealthy businessman, so she puts on well-tailored clothes and eats lunch in a well-to-do neighborhood around the large corporations. She settles in and meets new men to fill her date book with.

Preparing for Your Own "Prowl"

Let's say it's Monday evening and you've decided that Tuesday afternoon, during your lunch hour, you're going to look for a man. That evening write down what you're going to wear, where you're going, and the type of man you're looking for. Once you do that, you'll be in a mind frame that will be geared toward meeting a man.

Now it's time to identify a place where you will find your ideal man. The most important thing is the type of man that you're interested in meeting. Where does that man spend his time? What kind of job does he have? Let's say that you're interested in a man who is an engineer. You need to get a resource/phone book (as mentioned in Chapter 11) and look to see where engineers work in your area. Find a convenient location. During your lunch hour, go to that location. Find the office building and walk into a nearby restaurant. It can be a fast-food restaurant, a nice restaurant, a park—it doesn't matter. Whatever is located around the office building, that's where the men are going to eat. So, that's where you are likely to meet him.

As a side note, I have spoken to women who feel too nervous to eat when they are trying to meet men. Don't worry about it. You don't have to eat while you're looking. As a matter of fact, many people just drink coffee or a soda and do work if they are not hungry. So grab a soda and sit there while you look. Happy hunting!

How to Find a Man During His Lunch Hour: Outdoor Techniques

Many people find it relaxing to get outside and relax before they go back to work. Many successful businessmen, by the

way, don't have time to take a full lunch hour, so they sometimes walk outside and quickly eat a sandwich while sitting on
a bench. Otherwise, these men are not to be seen until after 6
or 7 in the evening. The following techniques can be used
when you are looking for a man outdoors at lunch time.

The Sack Lunch

Everywhere you go, you will see men sitting outside their work
buildings with a sack lunch on their laps. If you bring your
own sack lunch, then you will have to find a place to eat as
well, won't you? How convenient—there he waits, outside in
the sun, every day, dreaming of a wonderful partner who's
nowhere to be found. Day in and day out he sees the same people pass him on the sidewalk so that he no longer takes notice
of them. One day you arrive with your lunch in hand. His eyes
light up as he sees that God has sent him an angel. With that
in mind, how can he resist a friendly woman like you? He can't.

Follow the Leader

With this approach, you will find yourself waiting to follow a
man to lunch. What you do is simple. You sit in the lobby of
his building or outside the building near the door. You act as
though you are waiting for someone, until you see a man you
like. At that time you simply follow him to where he is going
for lunch. You have a built-in reason to talk to him too: "You
look familiar. Don't you work in the building across the street?"
It works like a charm.

A Walk in the Park

It's very common these days for men to go for a walk during
their lunch hour. Plan to sport your tennis shoes and walk at
least once a week during your lunch hour. Start outside your
workplace. This approach will expose you to men who work in
your own backyard. That should be followed by walking outside other buildings in your area. Remember, your goal is to

expose yourself to as many new men as you can, which increases your odds of meeting a man.

Your role is simple. When you see your man, say hello to
him and try to strike up a friendly conversation. If you don't
talk, make a note to yourself to walk next week at the same
time and in the same place you saw first saw him. He will be
there, especially if he found you to be his type. He could be
your date for next Saturday night—you never know.

How to Find a Man During His Lunch Hour: Indoor Techniques

The majority of men eat their lunches indoors, so here are
some ways to meet them on your lunch prowl.

Running Errands

Some men spend their lunch hours running errands while
women sit somewhere and eat. Most of the men who spend
their lunch time running errands are single men who don't
have a wife to do these chores for them. So, women, kill two
birds with one stone. Run your errands and pick up single men
as a reward for getting your chores done.

Meeting a Friend for Lunch

The lunch hour is a busy time in every office building. It is also
a good time to walk through the halls to see who the men are
who work in that building. When you see a man you are attracted to, you can ask him whether he knows where your
friend is working. You say that she works as a temporary secretary and said that she would be in that building that day. You
tell him that you are meeting her for lunch but can't seem to
find her. Of course, she isn't there, so you ask whether you can
use his telephone to call her. Call your own phone number and
leave a message for "her." When you get off the phone, you say,
"She probably stood me up again. I hate when she does that."

If you feel daring enough, you can say, "I hate to eat alone. Would you like to join me?" If the man is single and attracted to you, he won't be able to refuse.

Restaurant Sampling

The most popular day for people to go out to lunch is Friday. Take at least one lunch hour to sit down and eat lunch while looking for a man at the same time. Each week go alone to a different restaurant. As soon as you see a man you are interested in meeting, you now have a favorite restaurant for a couple of weeks. Begin eating there each week until you meet him. Keep in mind that you need to go alone. Men are less likely to flirt with you when you are with a friend.

Lunchroom Hopping

A lot of men eat inside their office buildings in the cafeteria. Don't miss this opportunity. These are typically men who don't meet a lot of women. They are busy and don't have the time or skill to look. The larger office buildings have lunchrooms in them. So keep an eye out for larger office buildings. During your lunch hour, once a week, pay a visit to one of the local lunchrooms.

Shopping at the Mall

Many malls have food courts that draw a variety of men during the lunch hour. Most of the men go there to grab a quick bite before shopping during their lunch hour. Always remember that people are creatures of habit and will return every week at the same time and place.

Dear Diary . . .
  While on a date last night, I noticed a man. He climbed into his car outside a small office building. Today, during

lunch, my curiosity got the best of me. I found myself in the same building pretending to be looking for my friend Darral. In all truth, I was in search of that man. There he was, behind a glass wall, in a meeting with another man. So handsome. So irresistible. With nothing to lose, I swung open the door, saying, "Excuse me, I'm looking for Darral." He stood up stating, "I'm Darral." Flattering him, I said, "You're more attractive than she is." Taking the matter seriously, the other man left in pursuit of Darral. Seizing the moment, I said, "You look familiar. Do you ever have dinner at the restaurant across the street?" Expected answer: "Yes, I was there last night." My response: "What a coincidence, so was I." The downfall came with his next comment: "With my wife." Ouch. A timely rescue by his boss as he walked in stating Darral was nowhere to be found. No surprise. I made a quick getaway thinking, "Maybe she's in the office next door?" I love adventure.

———————

14

How to Prepare
for the Catch

In this chapter you will find a man "source" sheet form. This sheet is a detailed sheet for your "search" activity. To remind you, the "search" is the time you dedicate to weekly flirting. Search time can be done at breakfast, lunch, or dinner. On this sheet you will simply write down your plan of attack: the activity (e.g., lunch), the place (local restaurant, park, etc.), where you are going to go to find the man, and the date and time you intend on going.

Keep These Points in Mind When Planning

1. Men, on average, go to lunch 15 to 20 minutes later than women. This little bit of information will help you avoid leaving the lunch places as men are arriving, giving you no time to meet them. So, if you can, leave a little later to lunch than you ordinarily would.

2. When it is your search time, do not schedule breakfast or lunch with a friend—go alone. Men are more likely to show interest in women when they are alone.

3. Sit close to the entrance of the place you go for lunch, if possible. This ensures that you will see and be seen by most of the men who walk in. Although you'll be sitting close to the

entrance, don't sit so close that men don't have anywhere to sit next to you.

4. Another good place to sit in a restaurant is near a customer focal point such as the telephone, restrooms, Coke refill station, condiment stand, or any other such customer area. This gives a man a good excuse to walk past you.

Creatures of Habit

People are creatures of habit. They tend to do the same thing day in and day out. This gives them some sort of organization to their lives. This is good for single women because it allows you to predict where men are going to be and what they are going to do.

Making Routine Changes

If you find yourself saying, "I never meet anyone new," it is probably because you are in a routine rut. By simply changing your routine, you will be exposed to many different men. It is very simple to alter your routine. Park your car in a different spot at work, walk in a different direction, change the day you go grocery shopping, or buy your morning coffee at a different place. It's very easy, and you will find it very rewarding due to all the new men who will come into your path in the process. Keeping all of this in mind, after you change your patterns, you will run into new men.

Save It for Later

If you see a man who interests you, store him, the time, and the place you saw him on your source sheet. He is a creature of habit. More than likely, he will be there at the exact same place and time the following week. This will allow you to write the event on your source sheet, put it in your calendar, and plan to "run into" him the following week.

Keep This in Mind

People don't like to change their routines, so typically they don't. You need to keep this in mind because you may find yourself resisting your own routine changes. Remember the rewards you will receive for making very simple adjustments in your schedule—MEN!

PROWL ATTACK SOURCE SHEET

Date _____

	Prowl Activity	Place	Date	Time
1.				
2.				
3.				
4.				
5.				
6.				
7.				
8.				
9.				
10.				
11.				

	Prowl Activity	Place	Date	Time
12.	_____	_____	_____	_____
	_____	_____	_____	_____
13.	_____	_____	_____	_____
	_____	_____	_____	_____
14.	_____	_____	_____	_____
	_____	_____	_____	_____

How to Use This Sheet

This page is a reminder sheet of the activities you will be engaging in to find a desirable man. Weekly, jot down your plan for the upcoming week.

Undercover Information

You can use this sheet in two ways: first, to help you remember to go back to see whether your creature-of-habit man returns; second, to summarize your Prince Charming search plan. Remember, you should schedule definite times in your weekly calendar to meet men: breakfast, lunch, or whenever. When planning, simply write down where you are going to go, on what day, and at what time. The reason for writing it down in your calendar is to make sure you follow through on it. At the end of each day (or week), jot down what you actually did along with notes about your successes. When you are first starting out, a success can be viewed as going somewhere new even if you decided not to flirt with the men there.

Important Facts to Record About Each Encounter

1. Name_____

2. Day_____

3. Time/Place_____

The Man's Attractive Qualities

1. _____
2. _____
3. _____

Potential Problems You Might Have with the Man

1. _____
2. _____
3. _____

Important Facts You Gathered About the Man

(e.g., how many children he has, his line of work, what he enjoys doing)

1. _____
2. _____
3. _____

Dear Diary . . .

The mist of my spell dangles in the air like a web waiting for movement to signal mealtime. I watch as his naive foot steps on my playground, setting the game in motion. Ritualistic entrapment begins. He'll do nicely. I drool at the menu item. His rippling body tempts the surface of my teeth. I imagine his mouth devouring my will and making me lose my inhibitions.

The force of my spell sucks the conscious awareness out of his mind. His eyes become glossy like a stunned doe. The electricity between us acts like a vein pumping an infectious disease into his being. It's terminal. There is no cure . . . only relief. He's mine.

15

How to
Approach a Man

In today's society, two factors prevent men from initiating conversations with attractive women: uncertainty about a woman's interest and fear of rejection. These are the very reasons that you need to use a little assertiveness to meet men. By "assertiveness," I am not referring to an all-out attack to get a man's attention; rather, I am talking about subtly using your ingenuity to meet him.

The majority of men do not like to be chased by women; they like to be the leader. In this chapter you will learn three ways to meet men. Each of the approaches varies from passive to aggressive, but in each, the woman leaves the pursuing up to the man. What you will be learning is the act of making a first move to facilitate a man's pursuit of you.

Think of all the times that you have wanted to meet someone but never did. There are also times when you see a man looking at you and you're returning the glances, but, in the end, each of you goes your own way.

Consider this story. Week after week, Carol ate Sunday brunch in a restaurant by herself. One day, Craig, a handsome attorney, sat four tables away from her. They were obviously attracted to each other. If he wasn't looking her way, she was glancing at him. They exchanged a couple of shy smiles but never met. For days Carol thought about Craig. For months she hoped he'd show up at the restaurant again. He never did. They never met. It was unfortunate, too, because they were each other's perfect type. Oh, well, that's what happens to those who hesitate.

It's frustrating and lonely to let so many eligible partners slip away just because you don't know how to meet them. Worse yet is the woman who refuses to meet a man because she expects him to meet her first. Let me tell you, that antiquated approach, which I call the passive approach, will get you nowhere. If you learn to make slight proactive changes, you won't have to experience what Carol and Craig did.

Sometimes men feel uncomfortable meeting a woman, so they let the attraction go by. Many men have told me that they welcome a woman who makes the first move. Men get tired of always having to be the initiators.

I want to make one thing clear here. Once you make contact with a man, it is important to step aside and let him pursue you. As you may know, men, by nature, like to be the leaders. When a man has to work to get a woman, it makes him want her more. If you take away the chase, you will take away his interest in you. So go ahead, make contact with him, but make him work to get you.

One last note. When you are in public and see an attractive man, keep in mind that no one in the entire place cares whether the two of you meet. No one is going to introduce the two of you. No one will say to the man, "Hey, there's a woman who looks like your type—why don't you go meet her?" No one will even notice that you are attracted to him. What I am saying is, if you see a man you want to meet, it will be up to you to meet him. If you don't make a move, then he will be another one who got away.

Now I want you to learn the three ways to meet a man. As you will see, most people use the least effective approach. However, don't fret—you will learn two alternative and highly effective ways to meet men.

The Passive Approach

Ninety-five percent of women use the so-called passive approach. By definition, this approach uses no initiative in the quest for a romantic partner. This passivity shows a lack of respect for your own needs. It communicates to men that you have a lower self-esteem because you don't go after what you want. To no surprise, many women who use this approach let the men in their environment dictate who will be their partner. Consider, for example, the woman who accepts a date with a man only because she "can't say no." Basically, these are the women who don't have the strength to break their repeating patterns that always end in unsatisfying relationships.

Women who fall into this category demonstrate their dating helplessness through statements such as "If I stop looking for a man, I will find one." This type of woman believes that she does not have to do anything to get a man. However, most women are unsatisfied with this approach because it maintains their no-dating status. They also find themselves settling for less than suitable partners. They know they deserve better, but it's too much work for them to make the necessary changes.

The main reason women continue this style of meeting men is because they are afraid of losing a man's approval. So, if you want more for yourself, you need to stop believing what you tell yourself: "I don't count; I let men take advantage of me; my feelings don't matter; my thoughts aren't important; no one wants me; I'm nothing." The next approach, "active," will teach you how to go after what you want and feel better about your choices.

The Active Approach

Five percent of women use this approach. This is the woman who takes some initiative in finding a partner, thereby dramatically increasing her odds of a successful search. An example of a woman who uses the active approach is the one who scrutinizes her past mistakes with men and decides what is now best for her. This means she steps out of her comfort zone of what she already does by doing something new.

This book is all about the active approach. From cover to cover you will read about new perspectives, different techniques, and self-education as ways of becoming more effective in meeting a mate. By incorporating something new, you will increase your odds of meeting a man. This can be any change, including learning what kind of physical and emotional type of man you are attracted to, using entrance lines to meet someone, learning to read basic body language, and/or following through on a plan to find a man.

There are three main reasons to use this approach. First, it will allow you to gain control over your dating situation. Second, you will have greater self-confidence, which will reduce insecurity and vulnerability. Lastly, the men you choose will result in closer, more emotionally satisfying relationships to meet your needs.

The Enthusiastic Approach

This is the most proactive approach of the three and, by far, the most effective. The woman who uses this approach is the one who takes risks, feels confident, knows the man she wants, and goes to the outer limits to meet him. Not all women are comfortable with this approach. As a matter of fact, I don't advise women to use this approach until they feels confident using the active approach first. Even then, she does not have to go to this extreme because the active approach is very effective.

Some women find it a challenge to go where most women don't go to meet a particular man. For example, Susan wanted to marry the president of a company. She went to the library and asked the librarian for help. She was directed to a reference book where she not only found the listings of hundreds of presidents but also their pictures. Susan was creative and contacted the companies and inquired about the marital status of each man she found attractive. Now Susan went to the extreme of flying to that state for a job interview just to meet the man.

Unfortunately, she didn't like him once she met him. As Susan demonstrates, some women can be enthusiastic and go to extremes to meet a man. But, as I say, if you have the time, self-confidence, and motivation, why not go to the extreme!

Summary

In closing this chapter, let me reiterate something about approaching a man in general. If a woman maintains a passive approach, she will continue in the rut she has always been in. If the woman decides to make slight changes, she progresses to the active approach and will see many changes in her dating life. For the woman who wants a real adventure, she can try the enthusiastic approach. What it all comes down to is being active. Any sort of activity creates movement toward finding a partner. Just remember—women usually begin using the passive approach but can get to the enthusiastic level with practice.

Dear Diary . . .

Steve. My date for tonight. Met in a bookstore. Hunted and caught. Piquing my interest, he progressed to date number one. Warning flags were all around when he suggested we meet at a country western club. I am not a fan of country music. Strike one. Having a bad attitude, I enter the club, climb up the stairs, and into the bar. There he sat, looking different than I had remembered. His suit gone. His power image stripped away and with that, my interest. Strike two. There he sat, in a western shirt, boots, and a cigarette. Strike three. Game over. You lose! Next batter!

16

How to Find His Faults Before You *Know* He's Wrong

Many women find themselves falling into patterns of getting involved with the "wrong" kind of man. This may prove to be frustrating, resulting in a helpless feeling. The question "Why?" is often asked. "Why do I keep getting involved with the same kind of men?" Well, let me tell you. It is because you aren't looking for early warning signs that signal you to get away. It might also mean that you are aware of the warning signs but rationalize their potential ramifications. Be that as it may, you are attracted to that "bad" trait or traits in men. Consequently, those characteristics lead to unhealthy relationships.

Many women find comfort in the familiar, even if it is bad. For example, how good do hot dogs really taste? They're terrible. Yet people eat them. This is because people ate them as children at ballparks and picnics. People associate wonderful, fun times with hot dogs. So, as adults, people eat hot dogs because of the wonderful memories they hold dear to them in their hearts from childhood. The same rule applies to relationships with men. Women may not necessarily like certain traits in men. But those traits bring back memories of something familiar. Therefore, they find safety and comfort in them.

How to Look for Early Warning Signs

The only way to avoid repeating harmful patterns is to be able to recognize the adverse signs early on. The earlier you see the signs, the easier it is to avoid getting hurt emotionally. Change is not comfortable. If you want to have a healthy relationship, you will have to learn to be attracted to a different type of man. I am not talking about a drastic change but rather a slight change.

To illustrate this point, Jennifer liked men who rode motorcycles. She enjoyed the camaraderie of the "gang" and the "bad boy" image. What she didn't like is that most of those bad boys were uneducated, unemployed drunks and unavailable emotionally. She finally compromised by hanging out in a "Rolex Biker Club." The men there were weekend bikers who played the part, except during the week they were successful businessmen.

Debbie's Bad Type

I consulted with a woman, Debbie, who continually became involved with emotionally abusive men. Certainly she did not like abuse, but it was her pattern. When she became aware of her pattern, she began to notice early warning signs such as possessiveness, rules of dress, and no tolerance for seeing family or friends. She decided she no longer wanted to be abused. She learned to end encounters with men immediately when she saw a red flag. For signs of an abusive man turn to the chapter, "Men to Avoid."

An Acronym to Help You

In this section, you will learn an easy way to remember your warning signs. If you have an unfavorable pattern of relationships, then you need to get as much information out of a man as fast as you can. You don't have to interrogate a man to get your questions answered, but you do need to be focused. The goal is to target your past issues or patterns to see whether the man you are talking with falls in that pattern. When a woman gets caught up in conversation with a man she likes, the conversation meanders through various topics, having no focus. The goal is to spend time with the man and nothing else. Go ahead and enjoy his company, except maximize your time by lightly discussing problem areas for you. The man will have no idea that you are discussing your issues. He will only think you are making conversation.

You can easily remember your problem areas by using an acronym.

An *acronym* is an easily remembered word formed from the first letters of a series of other words. The acronym used here is formed from the words and phrases indicating various potential problems a woman may have in relationships. Use these ideas or one of your own. It will be your way of remembering the focus areas to incorporate into conversations with new men.

This acronym is CONVERSATION:

C = Commitment phobic

O = Offspring

N = Not responsible

V = Verbal ability

E = Ethics/values

R = Religion

S = Sexuality

A = Addictions

T = Temper

I = Intelligence

O = Occupation

N = No money

How to Find a Healthy Relationship

To develop a healthy, lasting relationship, you must first qualify the man who interests you. You do this through observation
and conversation. Your goal is to screen for potential problems
that have ended your past romances. You can do this by observing the man carefully during your conversation with him.
This process is actually quite simple. I will take you through it
step by step so you have nothing to worry about.

List the problems you have had with men in the past (e.g.,
alcohol, temper, married, etc.):

Problem 1 _____

Problem 2 _____

Problem 3 _____

Problem 4 _____

Problem 5 _____

Now write down only the first letters of the problems (e.g.,
T, M, A). Write them here:

_____

Now see whether you can compose an acronym, a word,
using only those few letters (e.g., *A, T, M*—two possible words:
ATM and *mat*):

_____

_____

The Qualifying Process

You are now ready to qualify the men you meet, using both observation and conversation. From now on, when you observe
and talk with a man, try to cover each of the problem areas by
using your acronym. For example, Renee's acronym is *mat*,
which coincidentally is her ex-boyfriend's name. Renee is at the

movie theater and meets Harold. They strike up a conversation, and it's apparent there is a mutual attraction. Renee remembered to use her qualifying device when she watched Harold drinking heavily (screening through observation—A for alcohol consumption). Screening for marital status (M), she said, "This would be a great movie for children. My little girl would love it. Do you have any children?" His answer led him to explaining that he was having marital problems and contemplating divorce. Watching him guzzle another beer, she decided she knew plenty about this man and it was time to leave. As you can see, Renee saved herself a lot of heartache by not getting caught up in the euphoria of her infatuation. Instead, she directed the conversation to see if Harold qualified and he didn't. If she had followed the traditional style of romance, it may have taken her several weeks to discover what she unveiled in minutes.

Examples of Qualifying

It is actually very easy to qualify a man, as you read in the example with Renee and Harold. Like Renee, if heavy drinking has created problems in the past, pay attention to where you meet your men. Is it in a bar? If so, when you see a man you are attracted to in a bar, watch him a while before you meet (qualifying through observation). How much does he drink? Most heavy drinkers consume more than the average person without having signs of being tipsy. If you meet a man somewhere else, suggest meeting for predinner drinks on your first date. Watch for the same signs.

The married man. Observe him first. Do you see a wedding band? Does he give you every phone number except his home number? These are warning signs. If you see them, immediately end the encounter. You already know the ending—he'll stay with his wife and children and you will have no one. Save yourself some misery.

I'm sure you have the idea: make a point of finding the signs of the relationships that have gotten you into trouble in the past. Women are on a quest to find Mr. Right, so they tend to rationalize early symptoms in denial that he might be another "Mr. Wrong." Such rationalizations lead to the same result: a bad relationship.

———————

Dear Diary . . .
   There I was. Rubbing the magic lamp. A third wish? Experiencing cognitive impotence. I was distracted, baffled by my boyfriend's recent words of contradiction. He said one thing, but meant another. Did I misunderstand him? Last night he held me tight and said, "You must have been made to order; you're everything I want." This morning he left me a note which read, "I thank God for you every night." He loves me. Right? Wrong! This afternoon he broke up with me. I don't get it. My third wish? A voodoo doll and a sharp needle.

———————

17

How to Tell If He's Attracted to You

During a conversation, a man will look at a woman in one of three ways. The looks will vary from no attraction to strong attraction. Most men give no thought to how they are looking at you. Their eyes simply react naturally to their feelings. If a man is interested, his eyes will react differently to you than if he isn't interested. Here you will learn the types of looks a man will give you. It's very simple because there are only three types of looks to watch for.

Social Gaze

The social gaze is the typical eye contact most people use when they are having a conversation with someone they have no romantic feelings for. For example, this is the look a boss will give you during a conversation, the look a stewardess will give you, or anyone else to whom you are conveying thoughts to rather than feelings. Basically, this is a look in which the other person scans your eyes only, going back and forth from eye to eye. That's it. If you get that look, forget it. He does not view you romantically. But it does not mean that he won't eventually like you. Many people take time to warm up to someone to the point you can tell they are interested in you. If the friendship grows and he becomes interested in you, then his look will change to an intimate level, which is called the "intimate gaze."

Intimate Gaze

The intimate gaze is the social gaze plus something new. This is when a man looks at your eyes first, eye to eye. However, due to his curiosity and interest in you, he won't be able to resist caressing the rest of your face and hair as he talks to you. You will almost notice a slight distraction to his conversation, as though he's not quite paying attention, and he isn't—he's consumed with you. You will notice his eyes wander from your eyes, down to your lips, back to your eyes, to your neck, back to your eyes, and so on.

The distraction from your conversation comes from his subconscious attraction to you and possibly from his conscious awareness of you. As a side note, this is also the time you will notice the man touching you subtly, done with excuses such as taking lint off your shirt or an "accidental" touch of your hand followed by "You have cold hands." Any excuse will be used to touch you because the attraction is so strong.

Wow-Baby Gaze

The most intimate look a man will give a woman is the wow-baby gaze. This is not a lustful look. It is simply a look of captivation. This look encompasses the social gaze and the intimate gaze. It is the type of look you have when you experience "love at first sight," which is a look of complete intrigue. With this look you will see the man look at your eyes, your face, your hands, your clothes, your everything! He finds you so interesting that he is trying to gather as much information as he can about who you are in the shortest time possible. With this look, he will usually have a smitten expression on his face, which, obviously, is another sign of interest.

This phenomenon happened to Bridget when she met Dale. It was a cold day, and she was layered for warmth, not sex appeal. He seemed to watch her every move. He stared with captivation as she tied her boots; he curiously looked at her fingernails as she handed him a business card. It was one look after the other. There was no doubt in her mind that he was interested in her. Her insight was right. When a man seems fascinated, not lustful, he is very interested in getting to know you.

Let me make something clear here. It's not bad if a man looks lustfully at you, but a wow-baby gaze is a better indicator that he wants more than just sex from you.

Measuring Interest

By knowing the types of looks a man will use when he looks at you, it allows you to gauge how interested he is in you. Take, for instance, Loretta's friendship with John. She took a class at the local community college, and he was the teacher. As the semester went on, his looks changed along with his level of interest in her. Loretta was very interested in the class topic, so she spent time after class talking to John. Halfway through the semester, she noticed that he looked at her differently, using the intimate gaze. As his interest in her grew, he was so infatuated with her that his gaze progressed to the wow-baby type. The semester soon ended, and they began to date. For those of you who wonder—yes, she got an A in the class!

Many women worry that they will be conspicuous if they observe the way a man looks at them. Let me assure you, he will never know. To prove this, ask yourself how often you wonder whether a man is trying to read your subconscious thoughts as he has a conversation with you? You don't! Most people expect the person they are talking to to look at them. It's normal, so you have nothing to fret over. Go ahead and watch him looking at you.

How to Understand What His Eyes Are Saying

Certain things happen to a man when he is attracted to a woman. I am not talking about sexual arousal here; I am talking about sincere interest.

Women tend to keep a watchful eye on men they find attractive. By attractive, I don't mean physical appeal. Rather, I'm referring to a woman's idea of what she finds to be both physically and emotionally attractive. When a man is attracted to a woman, it will manifest physiologically in several ways. These ways are out of his control, and he is usually unaware that he is displaying them.

The Physiology of Attraction

Finding a mate isn't impossible. If it were, then humanity would have ceased to exist many years ago. Luckily, humans are biologically programmed to pair up with one another based on signs of attraction at a physiological level. Most people have no idea how attraction demonstrates itself in ways other than the obvious ways such as flirting, talking, smiling, and so on. Sometimes the so-called obvious signs are undetectable when a man is smitten with a woman. In most cases, it takes the reassurance of a girlfriend to let you know he likes you.

Men and women have a funny way of hiding the signs that they are attracted to each other. For some reason, people feel vulnerable when they let someone know their real level of interest. Most people play down their attraction in an attempt to keep a sense of control. It is all based on a person's fear of being rejected. To see through this smoke screen, all you have to do is look for the two signs of attraction that cannot be controlled. As a matter of fact, most people have no idea these signs of interest even exist. These two "secret" signs—dilated pupils and watery eyes—will give you the ultimate confidence that the man likes you if he exhibits them. I will get into details about each. For now, remember, a person can mask all of the physical and emotional signs of attraction, but he is unable to conceal physiological signs. Read about these two indicators, and you will have an advantage over the target of your interest. You will know he likes you, and he will be clueless.

Dilated Pupils

The first "secret" sign of physiological attraction is dilated pupils. The size of someone's pupil adjusts depending on three things: lightness, darkness, and attraction. If a man is in a darkly lit room, his pupils will enlarge. The opposite occurs when he is in a well-lit room: his pupils constrict. But when a man is attracted to you, his pupils will enlarge more than is expected for his surroundings. To find this out, simply compare his pupil size with others in the surroundings. If his pupils are large and everyone else has smaller pupils, guess what? That's right—he is attracted to you.

The eyes work like a camera lens. If they are dilated, more can be admired. If they are less dilated, the eyes aren't highly interested in what is before them.

A word of caution needs to be addressed here. Medications sometimes alter the size of the pupil. So if you think he's interested in you, but his pupil size is small, don't worry. All you need to do is watch for other signs of attraction such as body language.

Watery Eyes

Another physiological reaction a man has toward a woman he finds attractive is watery eyes. The eyes want a clearer picture of the desirable object so they tear to clean the lenses.

Gretta liked a man named Tom who, by the way, had a girlfriend. Even though she didn't pursue him because of this fact, her body still reacted with interest. Every time they spoke to each other, her eyes got so watery that she caught herself dabbing her eyes. One day Tom stated that she must be allergic to him because she always rubbed her eyes when they talked. Little did he know it wasn't an aversion but a positive emotional reaction to him.

Using the Secret Signs

Biology is in your favor when you are dying to find out whether someone is attracted to you. Take Janet. She was interested in her plastic surgeon but couldn't tell whether he was interested in her. He was outgoing and friendly with all of his patients, including her. After an appointment, he invited her into his office to talk and she noticed something different about him. When he looked at her, his eyes got so watery that he blinked a lot and turned away to dry his eyes. Then she noticed how dilated his pupils were. She was very surprised and delighted because she knew that he was interested in her. Later, after talking with his nurse, she confided in her about the doctor's interest in her. In the past she would have needed reassurance, but she saw his interest with her own eyes.

What Research Says

In research, when men were shown pictures of women with watery eyes and dilated pupils, they viewed them as more attractive than women whose eyes were not watery or dilated. So, you see, the natural act of demonstrating physiological attraction makes a person more attractive regardless of a person's rank on the 1-to-10 scale of looks.

Timing Is Everything

Single men, more often than women, are keenly aware of who's in their field of vision. Men, especially, are sensitive to the presence of women. Men tend to focus concentrated looks toward women of two types. The first is the grown-up Barbie doll who makes every man stare and drool. The second, and more important, type of woman a man tends to draw his attention to is the sort of woman he typically dates. Woman outside these two types of women will receive glances, at most. For women who fit a man's type, they will receive longer looks (two to six seconds or longer) and repeated looks. As for the Barbie doll women, all men look at them. However, the only men who date them are the ones who look like grown-up Ken dolls.

Lisa sits in an outdoor cafe. She notices that men glance at her at different distances away. Sometimes they look from a distance and don't look away. For others, they look at a distance, look away, and then look when they are up close to her. Lisa sees an attractive man looking at her, but she knows he's not interested because he doesn't look again once he is closer. Lisa's experience highlights what this section is all about.

There is definitely a set of unconscious rules that dictate when a man will look at a woman. With each rule, there is a clear meaning as to his level of interest in her. In this section, you will learn how to judge a man's interest in you by when he chooses to look your way. This judgment of interest is most accurate to measure when you are standing or sitting in a fixed place. Lisa, the woman in our example, was sitting in an outdoor cafe where she was visible to the men passing by.

How to Interpret the Distance of the Look

You can tell whether a man is attracted to you in several ways. In this section, you will be interpreting what a man's look means by how much distance there is between him and you. Before you get started with this interpretation, you need to mentally mark a few places in your environment. There will be three crucial markers, which I will explain shortly.

The first thing you need to do in your environment is to draw an imaginary line directly in front of you. Draw it in the direction of where people are walking by (refer to the chart here). Think of the imaginary line as a finish line, and you are the one holding the end of the rope for the contestants to pass to finish the race. Only in this race, the goal is not to cross the finish line, for crossing means losing the race. When you are either standing or sitting at a fixed place, you need to draw your "finish line" out from where you are. The second step is to visually mark another line five to six feet before that line. This line is called the "Attraction Line." The third line for you to mark off in your mind is the "Screening Line," which is 20 feet away from your "Finish Line." This chart shows what your imaginary field vision of vision will look like

You ——————————————————— "Finish Line"

5–6 feet away ————————————— "Attraction Line"

20 feet or more away ——————————— "Screening Line"

Screening Line

The screening line is usually the point in which a man will notice you. When you get a look from a man at this distance, it is nothing to be excited about. This is the first time a man sees you, so he's looking to see what you look like. It will take him 30 seconds to process whether you are his type or not. If the man likes what he sees, he will want to see you at a closer range. If this is the case, you will notice him looking at you longer than the typical stranger glance (one to two seconds). Instead, he will hold his stare for any amount of time. Men feel safe staring when they are at a distance because the distance is not an intimate range. Once the man reaches 20 feet from the finish line, he will turn his eyes away from you.

Attraction Line

The attraction line has important meaning. This is the line in which men decide whether they want to meet you. Remember, while they were at the screening line, they were checking you out. As they get to the attraction line, five to six feet away, they already know whether they find you attractive. If a man does not like you, it is very easy to tell. He simply won't look at you again, and he will continue past the finish line and lose the race.

The case of a man liking you is more interesting to watch. The attraction line for this man represents the time he is thinking of ways to meet you. You will see this manifested in sensible behaviors and nonsensible behaviors. The most common behavior is an unconscious avoidance of the finish line. For some reason, they know that it is too late to meet the woman if they pass that invisible line. Another action you will see is a sudden turn either in your direction or the exact opposite. At this time the man has not spoken to you because he is formulating his plan. For the man who turns the opposite direction to where you are, it is simply his way of gaining more time to figure out a way to meet you without making a fool of himself. He is almost guaranteed to come back your way once he has a couple of minutes to plan.

To demonstrate this point, take, for instance, Liza sitting in the lobby of a hotel. Little shops line the entire lobby across from where she is sitting. To the right of her finish line is the hotel cafe, which falls in the range of the attraction line. To the left of her finish line is the outside door. Off in the distance is Frank. He notices Liza, likes what he sees, and continues to look. He finally looks away as he moves closer to avoid looking too conspicuous. Finally, he moves to the attraction line and takes a very deliberate look, eye to eye with Liza. Suddenly, he takes a quick turn away from Liza and stops at a store window as though he's window shopping. He develops a plan of action. Once he's ready, he turns around, walks across the lobby, and reads the menu at the restaurant. Building up enough nerve, he walks over to the bench next to Liza and ostensibly gets something out of his briefcase. The reality here is that Frank was not window shopping or interested in eating at the cafe. His goal was to figure out how to get close enough to Liza to meet her. They struck up a conversation just as he planned he would.

For men who don't see you at the screening line, the chances of meeting are less because they haven't been allowed the processing time to see whether you are their type. When a man sees you for the first time when he enters the attraction line area, if he likes you, he will look at you a certain way. First, he will give you a "stranger glance" just because he notices a woman in his field of vision. Remember, this glance lasts only one to two seconds. If he likes you, he will immediately look at you again. At that time, he will go into the behaviors mentioned earlier that signal that he is attracted to you.

Finish Line

Regardless of attraction, if a man crosses the finish line, then your chance of meeting him is almost zero. Rarely, the man will turn back around and come your way, but don't count on it happening. Once the man passes, start looking for a different man, preferably at the screening line. The finish line is just that—a place to mark the end of a race.

"Why Does He Keep Looking at Me?"

When a person looks at you, it is simply a physical behavior brought on by an emotional thought or feeling (attraction to you or no attraction to you). Your chances of the man liking you are improved if he sees you at the screening line first, looks again at the attraction line, and avoids crossing the finish line. Refer to Chapter 19, "How to Convey Your Interest." That chapter will teach you how to let the man know you are interested in him so that he will make the next move, which is conversation.

"He Keeps Looking at Me. Does That Mean He Likes Me?"

Have you ever seen a man looking in your direction just to find yourself asking, "I wonder whether he's interested in me"? Women ask this question a lot. However, they rationalize that the man is simply looking in their direction and it means nothing. Wrong! Let me clear up this misconception right now.

First Look

If a man stares at you once, it only means that he sees a woman that interests him. It is also his way of seeing who else is in the room with him. The first look can vary in length, from a quick glance to a long stare, but it is nothing more at this point.

Second Look

If you catch the same man staring at you a second time, it means that he is attracted to you. He is also assessing whether you are his type and whether he is interested enough to consider smiling at you or approaching you. It takes women three seconds to size someone up and know whether she is interested in a man or not. Men are slow pokes. It takes them 30 seconds to reach the same conclusion.

Third Look

If the same man looks at you a third time, shout hooray! He likes you. The third look is the charm; it means that he has qualified you. You have passed his test and he wants to meet you. At this time he may do something to get you to notice him, such as walk past you. Most men will not take the initiative to meet a woman, so it is up to you to meet him. It may not sound fair, but if you wait for him to meet you, then you may never meet.

Men need "reasons" to approach women. So comment on something he has with him or something he's wearing. Men are afraid of getting rejected and of making fools out of themselves while doing the flirting dance. So try to make it a little easier for them. Remember, it's a chance you need to take to find a partner.

Fourth Look

If the same man is still glancing at you, it means one of two things. Reason 1: The man may be too shy to maintain eye contact or smile. If you want to meet him, you must take the initiative. Reason 2: Flirting with someone makes a person vulnerable. So, if the man is not flirting with you, then you need to examine what you are doing wrong. Are you conveying your interest in him? Refer to Chapter 21, "Guaranteed Entrance Lines." Is your body language saying you are interested?

Dear Diary . . .

I wanted to die today. All day, I prepared my mind to be able to expose my body at Howard's pool party. This was my big chance to finally meet Him. Howard.

At the poolside, I watched him take off his shirt and jump into the water. I was in heaven. It was my turn. I was going in after him. I stood there in shorts and a bathing suit top, not wanting to expose my bottom half. I'd better hurry, though, before he sees my cellulite. Ready to jump in. Off came the shorts! Down they went, past my thighs, past my knees, and down to my ankles.

Shock registered on the faces of everyone around. Suddenly a cool breeze hit my bottom—my bare bottom! I had somehow forgotten to put on my bikini bottoms! Reaching down to pull up my shorts, I saw Howard's face from the view I had between my legs. A big grin crossed his face, followed by insulting laughter. Knowing I could not hide, "Strike me dead, God!" I said. "Answer my prayer." That's the bare truth and nothing butt.

18

How to Master Nervousness

Have you ever had the experience of being attracted to a man but not having the nerve to meet him? Have you ever felt too uncomfortable to even look at an attractive man once he notices you? If you answered yes, you are not alone. Most of the women who have attended my seminars rank nervousness as their biggest problem when it comes to meeting men.

Flirting can be uncomfortable and embarrassing. Being nervous on top of this exacerbates the already uncomfortable situation.

The signs of nervousness are different for everyone. Jessica, for instance, hated going on dinner dates. She would get so nervous that her hands trembled, her mouth got dry, and her mind went blank. Try to imagine how uncomfortable she must have felt sitting across the table with a strange man: in need of moistening her dry mouth, she couldn't because her date would see her shaky hands. She finally learned how to deal with her nervousness and is now able to comfortably have dinner dates.

How to Get Over Nervousness

In this chapter, you will find eight ways to help deal with flirting nervousness. When you are nervous, your body will naturally give off body language that says that you are not interested in the men who are looking at you. When you feel uncomfortable, you want to cross your arms to soothe your nerves. Unfortunately, by giving in to your natural instincts, you turn men away. Don't fret. A solution to this problem is available, but it will take practice to change your patterns. Just keep in mind that dealing with your nervousness will make men view you as more approachable and thus more likely to flirt with you.

Signs of Nervousness

When a woman flirts, she makes herself vulnerable to rejection. No one wants to be rejected. Because of this, many women will not flirt even if they find themselves attracted to a man. Think of all the missed opportunities you have had in your past. The times when you were exposed to men you felt attracted to but never met. For most women, available men aren't lacking; rather, the confidence to meet the men they run into daily is lacking. It happens to everyone, and it is a shame that women feel too nervous to take the risk to meet those men. After reading this chapter, you will have proven techniques at your fingertips to help you meet all those men you have passed by in the past because of your nerves.

Attractive Aspects of Nervousness

Nervousness is not all bad. This list will enlighten you to the more positive aspects of nervousness:

1. It is natural to be nervous when meeting someone new. Men expect you to be nervous and find it flattering.
2. No one ever appears to others as nervous as she thinks she looks.
3. Nervousness goes away as you talk to that man.
4. The more experience you have with flirting, the more quickly your nervousness will subside.

Nervousness is simply a physiological reaction to the man you are attracted to. Don't view this response negatively, because you are reacting naturally. It's called "chemistry," and it's a magical feeling. It's also the basis of "love at first sight." The only time it isn't a good thing is when it persists and prevents you either from meeting men or communicating that you are interested in the ones you do meet.

Techniques for Dealing with Nervousness Around Men

The eight ways described here will help you overcome nervousness around men. Don't let your apprehension give the impression of a lack of interest. By controlling your nervousness, men will view you as more approachable.

1. Retreat

Definition: Leave the situation temporarily until anxiety subsides.

Example: Ellen is in the grocery store, and she sees Steve pushing his cart down the next aisle. She needs a few minutes to calm herself down, so she "retreats" by skipping an aisle and meeting up with him at another point in the store.

2. Talk to Another Person

Definition: Redirect your nervousness and conversation to someone you are not attracted to.

Example: Ellen joins a circle of people at a party. She sees Matt and feels too nervous to talk to him. To help get her mind off her anxious thoughts about him, she talks to Stuart who is standing next to him.

3. Move Around/Engage in Physical Activity

Definition: Force your body to move to discharge the extra energy nervousness creates (tie your shoelace, dig through your purse, walk to the bathroom, reach up to fix your hair, etc.).

Example: Ellen sees Dale, a new attorney in the monthly business meeting. Her tendency is to freeze up when she meets a man she likes. Instead of letting her nervousness build up, she releases it by *walking* to the drinking fountain to get a drink. By the time she walks back, the nervousness has subsided.

4. Perform a Simple Repetitive Activity

Definition: Distract your attention from the source of anxiety by focusing it on a task that requires simple, repetitive action (squeezing a stress ball, multiplying numbers by seven, chewing a piece of gum, snapping a rubber band against your wrist, tapping your foot to music, etc.).

Example: Ellen is too nervous to walk to the bathroom in the restaurant because it means having to pass a man she finds attractive. She puts a paper clip in her hand and counts how many snaps she does until she reaches the bathroom door.

5. Do Something That Requires Focused Concentration

Definition: Focus all of your attention on a task that demands your full concentration such as reading a book or magazine, solving a puzzle, writing a letter, playing a game, and so on.

Example: It's lunch time, and Ellen is in the local food court. She is sitting alone and feels uncomfortable because John keeps looking her way. To distract her attention, she writes a letter to her cousin.

6. Change Thought Patterns

Definition: Disrupt a pattern of negative or anxious thoughts by silently yelling, "Stop." The negative thought should be replaced by a positive statement.

Example: Ellen is having a conversation with Carl and thinks, "He must think I am so boring." Catching her thought, she yells (to herself, of course), "Stop" and replaces her thought with "I have so many interesting comments to add."

7. Practice Deep Breathing

Definition: Taking slow, deep breaths (minimum of three) to help anxious symptoms around men.

Example: Ellen feels tense when she sees Bill. Before approaching him, she pauses to take three deep breaths to release her nervousness.

8. Repeat Positive Statements

Definition: Anxiety leads to negative self-talk. Positive self-talk increases your self-esteem while calming you down at the same time.

Example: Ellen has gained seven pounds and feels unattractive. She sees Paul and thinks, "He wouldn't like me—I'm too fat." She catches her negative thought and replaces it with something more positive: "I sure look good in red; I bet he thinks I look pretty."

Managing Your Nerves

Although flirting is sometimes uncomfortable, you can learn to control your nervousness. Your body's reaction to nervousness is bad when it overrides your demonstration of attraction toward the man of interest. As a matter of fact, most women feel varying degrees of nervousness when they see a man they feel attracted to. This can be for a variety of reasons: the environment you are in, your confidence level, how you look that day, your state of mind, or anything that affects how you feel when you see the man. The point of the eight exercises is to redirect your attention away from your bodily reactions. Sometimes it only takes a minute to calm down; sometimes it takes a little longer. With practice, the discomfort stage becomes less and less.

Labeling Your Feelings

Many times women know that they feel nervous around men, but they don't know why. If you learn to identify what the feeling is, then you can combat your nervousness faster.

Self-conscious	Afraid	Desperate	Lonely
Panicky	Nervous	Depressed	Rejected
Sad	Threatened	Unattractive	Hurt
Hostile	Isolated	Jealous	Worried
Hopeless	Guilty	Foolish	Apprehensive
Disappointed	Burnt out	Inferior	Impatient
Insecure	Distrustful	Humiliated	Used
Incompetent	Useless	Tired	Pressured
Victimized	Ignored	Anxious	Outraged
Inhibited	Dirty	Helpless	Confused
Uncomfortable	Angry	Forgetful	Jittery

Once you label your feelings, you need to ask why you feel that way. Most of the time feelings are the result of negative self-statements of inferiority. In the next section, I list common negative thoughts many women have. As you will notice, several statements are about appearance or self-worth and result in any of the feelings listed. Many times these statements are generated because the woman believes them to be true or has experienced someone telling her they were true. In spite of that, women can learn to believe new things that are also true but positive. Keep in mind, like everything new, it takes a lot of practice before it becomes easier to do.

Words to Use

Here are two columns of statements, one with negative self-talk statements, the other with positive self-talk statements. Every time you catch yourself using a negative sentence, replace it with one of the lines in the right-hand column.

Negative Self-Talk	Positive Self-Talk
I am ugly.	I am pretty.
We have nothing in common.	I have interesting things to talk about.
I am fat.	Women should be curvy.
All I have to offer is sex.	I have opinions to offer.
I am too tall.	Men like tall models.
He doesn't like me.	Maybe I'm not his type.
I feel awkward.	I want to meet him.
I'm too shy.	Not everyone has to be bold.
I have nothing to offer.	I have a great voice.
He won't like me.	If he doesn't like me, that's okay.
I have an ugly body.	I'm good at camouflaging my flaws.
I'm too nervous.	I'll calm down soon.
No one likes me.	I need to like myself first.
I always say stupid things.	Everyone fumbles.
I'm too old for him.	He might be too young for me.
I'm not smart enough.	I have a great imagination and creative thinking.
I'm not perfect.	I bet he has flaws, too.
He only likes redheads.	He's interested in me.
Everyone uses me.	I won't let him use me.
I don't look good naked.	Candlelight makes me look good.

Challenging Negative Beliefs

Every time you have a negative thought, challenge it by asking the following questions:

1. "What evidence do I have for this belief?" Examine your life. Is there any truth to it?
2. "Is this belief always true? When isn't it true?"
3. "Does this belief promote good or bad feelings?"
4. "Did I choose this belief or did someone choose it for me?"
5. "What rewards do you get from thinking negatively?"

Many women find rewards for the negative thoughts they have. For instance, the woman who complains that she's too fat to find a date will get attention from people in the form of sympathy. Sympathy may be a reward, but wouldn't a change in thought be better, such as, "I'll find men who like big and beautiful women?"

If your negative beliefs aren't true, then you can change them. If you are always telling yourself bad things, then you will further damage your self-esteem. There is nothing more unattractive than a woman who feels badly about herself. If she doesn't like herself, then why should a man? To test this theory, the next time you are out in public, watch the women who get the most attention. It isn't the beauties; it's the women who project self-confidence. In the next chapter, I'll explain in more detail how you can learn to do just that.

Dear Diary . . .

"Thanks for joining me again," I think as I see him pushing his shopping cart down the cereal aisle. Monday after Monday, there he is. He's gorgeous and I want him. He's always so preoccupied, never noticing me. If only he'd lift his eyes from that wrinkled list he clutches each week. Oh, the tactics I've tried, inevitably failing with each one. Man-woman! Don't you get it? I am a woman; you are a man.

I should give up. However, the tactic this week—shattered glass on the hard floor—is guaranteed to work. Okay, I'm ready. Here he comes. Glass bottle ready in my hand. The drop! Oh, no! It didn't shatter. Just my luck—a plastic bottle. There he goes . . . around the corner. Another failed attempt. But stay tuned. Next week. Same time. Same place. New tactic.

19

How to Convey Your Interest

You learned in the last chapter how negative self-talk can damage your flirting skills. This exercise will help you in the flirting process. It will retrain your unsuccessful way of thinking.

When most women flirt, they have simultaneous self-defeating thoughts (e.g., "I'm probably too flat-chested for him to like me"). These thoughts distract from the flirting and make women self-conscious and thus more nervous. By eliminating the negative thoughts, you will be replacing them with new dialogue, a script for you to follow. This script will tell you exactly what to say, in the order to say things, and the appropriate time to say your lines. This new script may seem difficult at first, but once you replace your old grooves of thinking with new groves, it will become second nature.

Mental Tape-Playing Exercise

The next time you see a man you would like to meet, follow the three steps in this exercise:

1. Look (count to three, silently).
2. Smile (at the man).
3. Say hi (to the man).

Step 1

When you see a man who interests you, you need to engage him with a "look." If "looking" at a man isn't easy for you, then following directions will help you. The directions are self-prescribed. For example: Here comes your type of man. When he gets within six feet of you, repeat step 1 to yourself. However, don't just say, "Look." Yell *"look"* so loudly *inside your head* that you forget all other thoughts you are having. Many women tend to only "glance" at a man. A glance lasts only a second. When you "look" at a man, it needs to be at least three seconds. Looking at someone for three seconds seems like a long time. To help you though this uncomfortable time, you will need to count to three when you are looking at him: "one, two, three." Again, yell those words to yourself to block out your urge to turn away.

Step 2

Just looking at a man isn't going to assure him enough of your interest in him. More than likely, he won't take the risk of rejection by talking with you. Returning to the example in step 1, the man is approaching and you have given him your attention with a three-second look. Now follow the directions going on in your head and yell, *"smile!"* to yourself. A smile will follow. You're doing well! Now he is looking at you and returning a smile. You're on your way to meeting him.

Step 3

The most difficult part of meeting someone is saying your first word to him. The easiest word is usually "hi" or "hello." Back to our example: The man you are interested in is now looking at you, smiling at you, and if you follow this script, he will begin a conversation by saying, "Hello." Once again, you will have to tell yourself what to do next. The next step is to say, "Hi," so you yell the instructions to yourself *"hi!"* His natural response will be to say, "Hi." This simple word is sometimes all it takes to start a conversation with someone. It is also the most important of the three steps. Most men will not approach a woman if she only looks or just smiles. The word "hi" communicates interest the most to the man.

Practice Makes Perfect

If you are uncomfortable with this exercise, it is a good idea to rehearse it on men who are unappealing to you. The more practice you have, the more comfortable this process will become to you. Keep in mind the reason for following the script. It is to make the process of meeting a new man easy.

The script—steps 1, 2, and 3—will give you the format for meeting men. If each step is yelled inside your head, it will knock out competing thoughts that are negative in nature. Remember, negative thoughts lead to increased nervousness.

This exercise is only the first step to meeting a man. It acts as an icebreaker that gives each of you an "excuse" to talk. Refer to Chapter 21, " Guaranteed Entrance Lines," to teach you the words to say after "Hello."

Dear Diary . . .

Hindsight couldn't have predicted this. My professor teased me . . . I teased him back. He hinted. I followed his lead. I delivered a proposition in note form, suggesting coffee after class. His face turned red. I was tickled pink.

Without question he gave me his answer. My pink shade turned red with surprise as I watched him torture my invitation, then casually toss it aside. There, on his desk . . . My crumpled note sat quietly humiliated before a class. As blatant as a scarlet letter to some, as unnoticeable as the Emperor's clothing to others.

20

How to Interpret Body Language

Before you talk with a man, you *see* him. The mere sight of an attractive man causes an emotional reaction. What follows is an unconscious adjustment in your body language. Ideally, the body will communicate openness, approachability, and warmness. This reaction would, in turn, unconsciously invite the man over to meet you. In reality, nervousness gets factored into this equation, along with "playing hard to get" and fear of rejection. Unfortunately, all of these act as agents to detour the man from meeting you.

How Men and Women Communicate

People communicate in three ways:

70 percent through body language

23 percent through tone of voice

7 percent through the words actually spoken

It is interesting that most people are concerned with what to say to someone they are interested in when, in fact, their concern should be in how they say it. As you can see, 93 percent of a person's communication is conveyed through body language and tone of voice.

If you train yourself to watch for certain behaviors, you will immediately be able to tell whether a man is interested in you or not. Knowledge of these behaviors will allow you to prevent taking unnecessary risks of being rejected by talking to men who aren't interested in you. It is also important to pay attention to your own body language to see whether you are communicating an accurate message to men.

Ten Giveaway "Actions" That He's Attracted to You

1. He will touch you.
2. He will invade your personal space.
3. He will ask you personal questions.
4. He will look at you more than once.
5. He will look at you longer than three seconds at a time.
6. In conversation with others, he will maintain eye contact with you more than anyone else.
7. He will compliment you.
8. He will smile more at you than anyone else around.
9. His gestures will be exaggerated around you.
10. His voice will have more variety in terms of volume, tone, and expression around you.

Helen was interested in Dale, a graduate classmate of hers. She was confused and couldn't tell whether he liked her too. One day during a study group, she observed his body language and was delighted by what she saw. First, he sat next to her. He also sat much closer to her than to the person on his other side. The real giveaway was when he touched her hand three times as he pointed to things in her textbook. When he spoke, his eyes were on her more than anyone else. It was one clue after another, adding up to the fact that he was interested in her.

Many women are afraid to take the risk of letting a man know they are interested in them unless they know the man has interest. Like Helen, once she noticed Dale's interest in her, she let her wall down and showed interest in him. She conveyed her interest the same way he did—by using the 10 giveaways.

Meanings of Body Language

The process of communication is a combination of nonverbal and verbal. Behavior expresses meaning more clearly than words. To understand a man more fully, you need to pay attention to his body language. You need to train yourself to look for the signs of interest in terms of "actions" and "body signs." Actions are sometimes deliberately done to show interest, but body signs are more subconscious. These signs work as an automatic reflex in response to attraction. When someone is attracted to another, there is a natural urge to get as close to that person as possible. Craig put it this way: "When I like a woman, all I want to do is get close to her, to smell her hair, her perfume, to lightly brush her hand. It feels like a driving force behind my conscious thoughts."

In the previous section, you learned which nonverbal "actions" to watch for that communicate interest. Now you will learn the more subtle forms of attraction from body signs. They are easy to spot once you are aware of them.

Fifteen Body Signs That Show His Interest

1. He will lean forward.
2. The front of his body will face you directly.
3. He will tilt his head.
4. He will sit on the edge of his chair to get closer to you.
5. He will touch his face often, especially as he looks at you.
6. He will smile either at you or to himself when you are around. This is an unconscious way for him to look appealing and draw attention to himself.
7. He will display grooming behaviors (slick his hair down, straighten his tie, check his teeth).
8. He will exaggerate body movements to get you to notice him—for instance, expansive gestures, waving arms.
9. He will moisten his lips.
10. He will play with his clothes.

11. He will touch you briefly, accidently or on purpose.
12. He will laugh or clear his throat to get your attention.
13. He will look at your mouth not just your eyes when he talks to you. This type of look is more than a glance. Men have told me that they look at a woman's mouth and imagine kissing her.
14. If he crosses his leg, it will be in your direction.
15. He will sit or stand within six feet of where you are. This makes him close enough to say something to you.

All these body signs have three unconscious motives behind them from the man's point of view: to get as close to the woman as possible, to draw attention to himself, and to make himself look his best by grooming himself.

"I've Known Him So Long— How Can I Tell If He Likes Me?"

Many times men and women establish longtime platonic friendships that never turn to intimacy even though there is an attraction between the two. This can happen for a variety of reasons. Perhaps one or both are already in a relationship, or it doesn't seem appropriate to pursue a romantic relationship for some reason. Sometime there comes a time when you want to change the relationship to make it intimate. Or, you've never really known whether the man was interested in you, but you're curious because you are interested in him romantically. This situation is especially common in the workplace when you work with a man for years but nothing romantic materializes.

Courtship progresses through three distinct stages of nonverbal intimacy. The following section will help those women who have been attracted to a man for a long time but can't tell whether he is seriously interested in her. It can also be applied to a woman who is interested in a man she has a platonic relationship with and wants to test the water to see whether something more could be there if she pursued it.

The mystery can now be solved. Here are the stages people
go through that demonstrate levels of interest.

Stage 1: Qualifying Mates—Glance to Look

Glances between strangers hold no meaning. Glances are a way
of observing your environment. When the glance becomes a
look, it takes on new meaning and holds a lot of importance.
Looks act as an investigative team, searching for details about
a person. Looks come out of curiosity about someone. Looks
are the first step toward a romantic relationship.

Stage 2: Eye Contact—Nonintimate to Intimate

When people share eye contact, it furthers the level of intimacy.
If you will notice, friends give each other short looks during
conversations, but couples stare into each other's eyes. If the
man you are interested in always engages you in eye contact, it
acts as a signal that he would like to become more acquainted.

Stage 3: Conversation—Superficial to Personal

Typical conversations between friends are trivial and superficial. They act as a character-defining stage for each to get to
know the other. If each person decides they are compatible,
then the conversation will become personal and more deeply
involved. A man doesn't ordinarily share secrets with a woman
unless he is emotionally involved with her.

Stage 4: Touch—Platonic to Romantic

Nonromantic touch is usually the first sign of intimacy. This is
a point that allows either of the individuals to withdraw from
the friendship without rejecting the other. However, if it continues, it leads to romantic touch. Initial touches are brief and
few. Later touches are more deliberate and longer, such as the
man who leaves his hand on your forearm while he emphasizes
a point in his conversation.

Stage 5: Touch—Friendship to Intimate

This stage of touch is still noncommittal, meaning that neither person has verbally said they are romantically interested in the other. A friendship touch is done without the body touching and is not face to face. When intimate thoughts are behind the touch, you will receive body touches such as long hugs. These are not the type you give to a friend. Light kisses might also occur. The second a man holds your hand while you walk, or puts his arm out for you to hold, or gives you a kiss of any kind (even kissing a cut on your hand), it means he is romantically interested in you. This is the perfect time to do something to change the relationship because he feels close to you.

When Becky liked Mario, she made the biggest impact on him when she kissed him. Previous to that she had been his support person through his tumultuous relationship with his girlfriend. One day at work Mario complained that he had to do laundry that night. She suggested he come over to her house and they do theirs together and have dinner. Up to this point, nothing romantically had ever taken place between the two of them. In the middle of dinner, Becky's phone rang, and it was Mario's histrionic girlfriend with another one of her "rescue" calls. Becky got wise and planted a long kiss on Mario's lips as he left to help his girlfriend. Mario later told her that he couldn't stop thinking about her from that moment on.

A Change of Scene

One reason that people continue to view the person platonically is due to the associated environment. Well, the fastest way to change a person's perspective of you is to get them out of that place and into a romantic setting. Take Melinda, for instance. She played tennis with Jim for years. This tennis partnership began before her marriage, during her marriage, and after her divorce. One day she looked at him differently. He was so handsome to her. For some reason, on that day she saw him as a man, not a tennis partner. As the days went on, her tennis outfits became more feminine and revealing and their conversations lingered after each game. She decided to suggest getting a drink after one game, and the whole relationship changed. He said yes but wanted to take a shower first. That was perfect. It gave her a chance for him to see her in a different light. They met at a local restaurant, and "drinks" turned into dinner. She later commented on how he lit up when he saw her walk into the restaurant in a great dress. He didn't take his eyes off her all night. Tennis was never the same for them again.

Take the example of Melinda and Jim and do what Melinda did: take the man you are interested in out of the usual environment he sees you in. If you make the place a romantic environment, his perspective of you will take on a new association.

Ways to Change a Man's View of You

It is a good idea to gradually change the nature of the relationship. In each of the suggestions given in this section, always tie your invitation to the environment you are already in or to something nonthreatening. Take Joyce, for instance, who was attracted to her college professor but didn't think it was appropriate to flirt with him. Instead, she waited until the end of the semester to make her move. She went to his office to pick up her test. Fortunately, for the sake of romance, she didn't do well on the test. She asked if her teacher would mind going over a few of the questions with her. After 10 minutes, she told him that she was too hungry to concentrate and asked whether they could go to the cafeteria to discuss the test while she ate. He gave in, and, like the example with Melinda and Jim, their conversation eventually turned personal. Many more conversations followed that were off campus.

Here are some ideas on how to change a man's perspective of you:

- Call him at home to ask him a question about something the two of you have in common already. Let that conversation wander into a personal nature.

- Suggest getting together for a drink.
- Ask him to do a favor, such as helping you move a heavy piece of furniture at your place.
- Tell him that you are cooking a special dinner and need someone to taste-test it for you. Of course, he has to go to your house for the tasting.
- Ask him to drive you home because your car is in the shop.
- Tell him you need to stop by his place on your way home because a personal package was given to you by mistake and you'd like to drop it off. Put together something at that time in an envelope with his name on it. Remember to act clueless. The key is to get into his house and spend time together.
- Tell him you need his opinion about something, but want to meet elsewhere so no one will hear.
- Draw out your conversations. If you're at work, stop at his desk near the end of work and get into a serious conversation that needs to continue longer.
- Turn your conversations away from work or whatever you ordinarily talk about and make it personal. Get him to talk about himself, stories of childhood, past relationships, and so forth.

Sometimes women think they have to go "out" to find a partner when in fact they may already know a great man. Sometimes a change of perspective about a man can suddenly turn a friendship into a romantic relationship. Changing someone's perspective about you or changing your view of someone might take a long time, particularly if it wasn't romantic to begin with. The more often you change the content of your conversations or the environment you spend time in, the faster the relationship will change.

Go Away! How to Convey When You Are Not Interested

Nonverbal actions communicate all sorts of messages, good and bad. Single women learn to communicate nonverbally,

especially when they need to communicate something unfavorable to a man. A good example of how powerful a nonverbal message can be was demonstrated in the diary entry for the
last chapter. The man who received the note responded with a
blatant "I'm not interested in you" by crumbling the note. In
this section, you will find other ways to let a man know that
you are not interested in him by using body language and nonverbal communication.

Ten Nonverbal Ways of Communicating Dislike

1. Stare, glare, jitter, or avoid eye contact.
2. Speak too softly.
3. Use a disinterested tone in your voice.
4. Be sarcastic.
5. Agree with everything he has to say.
6. Yawn, frown, or simply have a blank expression.
7. Lean away from him.
8. Cross your arms.
9. Move away from him.
10. Stand more than four feet away from him.

The point you must get across is that you have no interest in
being close to the man, whether physically, emotionally, or
spiritually. A word of caution needs to be given here. If you engage in one or more of these behaviors, you may inadvertently
convey disinterest to a man. So if you are interested, refrain
from any of the negative behaviors listed here. On the other
hand, if you have no interest, combining a couple of negatives
will get rid of the unwanted, even the most obtuse, pretty
quickly.

Dear Diary . . .
    The best time to meet men at a grocery store is 6 P.M.
*I push my shopping cart toward the man thumping a water-
melon. I say, "Don't I know you from somewhere?" just to
hear his wife call, "Honey!" Okay, so it didn't go so well. I*

move on to another man near the bakery. Confidently, I ask, "Do you have the time?" Before he gets a chance to answer, I hear the name "Daddy" being screeched from four unruly children running in his direction. I'm persistent. I move on to a man examining chicken breasts. "You seem fickle—you must be a Taurus." Turning toward me, I notice his T-shirt: "Gay Rights." With egg on my face, I quickly apologize, saying "I thought you were my boyfriend." Boyfriend? He's the one who has a boyfriend. Oh well, maybe next week I'll fare better.

21

Guaranteed
Entrance Lines

Communication has to start somewhere. Entrance lines are introductory sentences you use to talk to a stranger. If there is a mutual attraction between two people, then it does not matter what you say. Each of you will recognize an attempt to meet each other.

The No-Fail Approach to the Entrance Line

By far the most successful entrance line is a question. No one can refuse to answer a question. This allows you the opportunity to meet the man you want without having to rely on traditional flirting. There are three steps in asking a man a question:

1. Say, "Excuse me."
2. Ask an open-ended question.
3. Give a follow-up statement after he responds that is personal in nature.

Open-Ended Questions

When you ask a man a question, make sure it is an open-ended question. This means that the answer cannot be answered with

154

a yes or no response. Open-ended questions allow people to answer on their own terms—who, what, where, when, why, and how. The goal of communicating this way is to initiate a real conversation. Ask questions that will lead to conversation. Also, keep in mind that any contact is best received when you approach the person with a smile, full eye contact, and a clear, audible voice.

The Goal of the Question

Remember, one of your goals is to find out as much as possible about the man early on to avoid the rut of an unsatisfactory relationship. By asking questions that elicit detailed responses, you get a lot of information up front.

A lot of people are under the mistaken impression that, when you're talking, you're in control. That's not true. When you ask the questions, you are in control. It allows you to direct the path of the conversation.

Another advantage to asking questions is that people like people who are interested in them. Keep in mind your main aim. You want to know if he qualifies.

Entrance Lines

Any line can be used, even the traditional ones such as "Don't I know you from somewhere?" Listed here are lots of lines to use. Having several opening lines handy can help alleviate anxiety, freeing up energy for conversation.

1. What time do you have?
2. I can't believe the news coverage on _____. What's your opinion?
3. Who are you rooting for?
4. I'm lost. Do you know where _____ is?
5. Have you ever heard of _____? Do you know where it is?
6. Weren't you at _____'s party a couple of weeks ago?

7. Are you waiting for someone? I hate to sit alone, would you mind if I sit next to you?
8. Which frozen pizza do you think is the best?
9. Do you have change for a dollar?
10. Do you know when the rain is supposed to start?
11. Do you know where the local food court is?
12. I'm looking for a pay phone. Do you know where one is?
13. I'm terrible with directions. Can you draw a map for me?
14. May I borrow your phone?
15. While writing a letter, ask a man how to spell a certain word.
16. Make casual observations: "That salad looks delicious."
17. Offer something: "Would you like to read this newspaper?"

Men love flattery and compliments, so don't hesitate to walk directly up to a man and comment on what you find attractive about him. The key to success is delivering a genuine and wholesome compliment, such as "You have the most beautiful eyes. I couldn't help noticing you." "You look so smart. I just had to say hi." "Your smile lights up the whole room." The typical response to entrance lines like these will be a big smile and a little embarrassed blushing.

Overall, for an entrance line to be successful, you need to comment on your surroundings. If you are in an office building complex, you can ask for directions to an address, pay telephone, building manager, local restaurants, coffee shops, copy center, and so on. If you are in a grocery store, ask the man what kind of lettuce is best for a Caesar salad. Basically, make your question or entrance line believable. When people get nervous, they sometimes forget this and ask questions that don't make sense to the person they are directing it to.

Entrance Line Examples

Example 1: In the Grocery Store Parking Lot

Woman: Excuse me. (step 1 of the "no-fail" approach)
Man: Yes?

Woman: Do you know where the nearest ice cream store is? (step 2).

Man: It's three blocks away in that direction.

Woman: I've been craving ice cream all week. Which ice cream place nearby do you think has the best ice cream? (step 3)

Man: Sure, _____ is across the street.

Example 2: At the Library

Woman: Excuse me. (step 1)

Man: Yes?

Woman: That looks like a good book. The title sounds familiar. Is it worth checking out? (step 2)

Man: Well, it's OK, but there is one section where . . . ."

Woman: "That's an insightful observation." (step 3)

Do you see what I mean? Meeting someone by using entrance lines can be easy if you make it simple. Regardless of whether this woman likes the book, this process is going to keep the interaction going. Remember, the point is to meet the man and give him an excuse to talk to you.

Manipulating the Intimacy of Conversations: What to Say If You Like Him

If you find that the man qualifies, then it's time to change the tone of the conversation to a personal nature:

1. Start out by talking about superficial topics.
2. Use words that are thinking or cognitive in nature.
3. Move to conversation that is personal in nature.
4. Move to words that use feelings.

Let's consider each of these in a bit more detail.

Step 1: Superficial Topics Superficial topics are general or broad statements about any subject. They are no-brainer subjects that anyone can discuss such as the weather, a hot topic in the news, the president, the surroundings, a restaurant you just tried, last night's storm or earthquake, and so on.

Step 2: Thinking Words   Thinking words are the opposite of feeling words. They have no emotion to them. They are factual and don't elicit much of a response. They are nonthreatening words to use at first to start a conversation off, such as "I've never thought of it that way." For more examples, turn to Chapter 24 on exit lines.

Step 3: Personal Conversation   Personal conversation is the opposite of superficial topics. These are areas related to the person on a specific topic, rather than on a broad level. This goal is to disclose something personal about your past, present, or future. It can be anything from where you were born to what your favorite hobby is. Such a statement causes the other person in the conversation to reciprocate. Personal conversation leads to bonding between people. If self-disclosure comes from the man first, it means that he is attracted to you.

Step 4: Feeling Words   Feeling words create an emotional reaction in a person. These reactions can be tied to any emotions: anger, jealousy, joy, sadness, fatigue, and so on. You use these words to speak at a level of closeness. For example: "That smell brings back such warm childhood memories." For more examples, turn to Chapter 24 on exit lines.

Putting It All Together: Example Conversation

   Woman: Excuse me. Do you know who is in charge here (superficial topic)?
   Man: No. I think the manager's office is down the hall.
   Woman: I have never been here—will you show me the way? I feel "uncomfortable" in new places (feeling word).
   Man: Sure, I'll show you.

Woman: You are so nice for showing me the way. Are you in a helping profession? You remind me of my father—he always goes out of his way to help lost people (personal conversation).

What to Say If You Don't Like Him

Your goal in conversation, like always, is to qualify men to find a suitable mate. This means that you will be looking for red flags that indicate for you to end the conversation and move on to a new candidate. In that case, you will want to do the following:

1. Return to conversation of superficial topics rather than personal topics.
2. Return to using thinking words rather than feeling words.

When you end a conversation, you can do it very quickly by getting away from the personal and feeling level. There is no need to be rude. For more details on how to end a conversation, turn to Chapter 24, "Graceful Exit Lines."

Sometimes the past offers us new ways of how to get a man to woo us. Take the Victorian period, for example. When a girl was interested in a man, she was the one to ask him to "call" on her. It was viewed as highly improper for the man to take the initiative. This "calling on" either led to marriage or of being viewed as an unsuitable partner. In that case, when men came to call on the woman, they were given "excuses" as to why the woman could not accept their call. The man eventually got the hint that he was unwanted and stopped pursuing her.

Example Conversation

Man: My father gave me this watch. I remember that day so well. . . .

Woman: It really is a unique watch. Thank you for telling me its history. I really do need to get back to the office. I'm expecting a call.

Dear Diary . . . .

    Reality slipped away as I entered the mansion doors in my sexy black dress. The house was filled with beautiful people. I stood there, locked in an "across the room" gaze with Paul. The force of our attraction was spoken like braille to the fingertips in blind darkness. No one felt this but us. But it didn't matter.

    He followed me as I entered the cave beneath the waterfall next to the pool. The heat of the Jacuzzi only added to the fire between us. Not having a word to say, I laid my hand on his tie, I pulled him close, and placed my lips to his. I saw stars as I heard the fireworks going off in his head.

    To add to the drama of our first meeting, away from him I moved . . . out into the party again. Never a word spoken. Just spontaneous intimacy.

22

When You're Tongue-Tied, Try an Entrance *Action*

You can have a verbal encounter with a man in two ways. One, as discussed in Chapter 21, is through entrance lines. The other way is through entrance actions. Entrance actions allow you to converse with a man through behavior. In the diary entry for the last chapter, as you read, sometimes an entrance action can be very bold, such as an unsuspected kiss. I don't advise this for everyone, but it's okay to get a little crazy now and then.

Benefits of Entrance Actions

Do you remember back in grade school how much fun it was to give boys love notes? Well, entrance actions allow you to have that same thrill by doing playful actions. The great part about entrance actions is that they add suspense, curiosity, and intrigue to the woman doing these things. It will make an impressive impact on the man because it will set you apart from all the other women.

Even shy women can use entrance actions. As a matter of fact, many women I have met through my seminars have had great successes using the items listed later. Take Torrie, who was very attracted to Tylor but was too shy to meet him. She decided to put a Kiss candy on his desk at work every day. She replaced the kiss paper inside the wrapper with her own slip of paper. Of course, she put a note on the paper. The first day the note read, "You have a secret admirer." The subsequent notes gave clues to who she was—hair color, height, weight, and so on.

Entrance Actions: Examples

News Flash

When you see a man reading a newspaper, become interested in an article or picture and get caught reading his paper. You can also ask him whether there is anything interesting in the news today.

Mail Carrier

Mail him a blank envelope scented with perfume. This will arouse curiosity.

The Candy Man

Put a Kiss candy on his desk (or mail it to him). Replace the kiss paper with your own note, such as "May be redeemed by Cinderella."

Recycling

Say to him, "Excuse me. Do you have a piece of paper I can borrow?" Take the paper, write your name and phone number on it, hand it back to him, and say, "Never mind, I don't need it anymore."

Bumper Cars

"Accidentally" bump into him when you see him. This means reaching across to get something (a straw at lunch time) and bumping him as you do this. You can also pretend to be reading a book or paper and run directly into him. Anytime you go into someone's personal zone, it gives them a rush because it is unexpected.

Traffic Cop

Find a piece of paper in the size and shape of a ticket and put it on his car window. To add to the suspense, you can put one on his car each day, along with a different number to your phone number. At the end of seven days he will call.

The Great Paper Chase

Drop something when you get next to him, such as papers or change. If he's any kind of a gentleman, he will help you pick it up.

Lunch Prowl

Eat lunch in a different office building a couple times a week to meet men you don't ordinarily meet.

His Lucky Day

Send him a fortune cookie with your own special note tucked inside.

The Handshake

When giving a handshake, keep one point in mind. The average shake lasts as long as the cordial greeting words last, such as "It's nice to meet you." If you let your hand linger a second or two longer, it will send a powerful message of interest to the man.

Lunchtime Surprise

Send him a note in a restaurant through the waiter. For note ideas, turn to Chapter 23, "How to Be a Secret Admirer."

The Office Visit

Once a week go into a different office building and scout the offices for your type of man. Walk directly into his office and ask him whether he knows where someone or something is. Tell him that your friend is a temporary secretary and is working in his building today.

Follow the Leader

At lunch time, look for your type of man and follow him to lunch. Another version of this is to follow him after lunch to see where he works. The next day you can pay him an office visit.

A Few Other Ideas

1. Walk over to him with a small item and ask whether it belongs to him.
2. Take lint off his shirt.
3. Touch the material on his sleeve and comment about the material.
4. Follow him and continue to run into him.

When using entrance actions, try to make them as creative as you can. Impress him by your uniqueness and win his heart with your charm. Anything that causes you to stand out from the other single women is advantageous to you.

The Special Effects of a Touch

When you are flirting, try to touch the man in a nonthreatening manner on the wrist, forearm, or hand. Research shows that touch has a powerful effect on a stranger's perceptions of you. Touchers tend to be viewed as warm, caring, kind, loving, and exhibit other positive characteristics. So keep in mind, when you touch a man, it hits him on a physical level as well as an emotional level.

Recently, Doug told me how a touch from his girlfriend Diana made a dramatic alteration in his attraction to her. For months

Doug casually spoke to Diana at church without much chemistry. Diana, on the other hand, thought he was the most beautiful man in the world and wanted to date him. Well, Diana made her wish come true the day she deliberately put her hand on his forearm during a conversation. Doug said he instantly viewed her differently and couldn't wait to see her at church each week. He attributes his attraction to her touch, which opened his eyes to her pretty face. They are married now and Doug lives happily with many touches by his beloved Diana.

Don't underestimate the power of touch. If you find a man attractive, go out of your way to touch him.

What to Say in a Secret Admirer Note

Secret admirer notes are simple to write. These notes can be as creative or as plain as you would like. If you are a creative person, have fun and go all-out. If you lack creativity, a simple note, following the guidelines here, will convey the same message and get the same response.

Note 1: *"You have a secret admirer; there are more clues to come."* This letter informs him that someone is attracted to him. It also makes him anticipate your next note.

Note 2: *"Clue 1: I have _____ (blond, red, black, whatever) hair. Have you guessed yet?"* This note is a hard note to send because it gives away your identity a little. But send it anyway because you want to meet him.

Note 3: *"Clue 2: I am _____ (state height). Are you curious yet?"* This note will drive him crazy. He will begin to put a lot of energy into revealing your identity.

Note 4: *"Clue 3: The eyes that watch you are _____ (eye color). By the way, I love your _____ (eyes, smile, etc.)."* This letter is a good time to give him a compliment.

Note 5: This letter should reveal an obvious clue as to your identity. By this time, the man will be flattered by your pursuit. If you send this note, you have to be sure that you want to meet him.

Alexandra went on a campaign one time to meet an attorney who worked in an aerospace company. Each Wednesday she attended a public speaking class called Toast Masters. One day she noticed Brandon, who worked in the corner office. He was so handsome, but she didn't know how to get him out of his office. She did some research and discovered his name. She decided to get him to meet her by sending him an anonymous note. The first note read, "I'm curious about you!" The weeks went by and she sent a dead giveaway note that read, "I am in your building every Wednesday at 4:30 P.M.—look for me next week." The next week came and there he was, out of his office, right in her path. She smiled as she walked by—it was 4:30. No response! After her meeting, she felt a little frustrated. She passed by his office, and he looked at her as she looked at him. Still nothing. Feeling bold, she turned around, walked over to his office door, and asked, "Have you received any interesting mail lately?" He started to laugh, "It's you? I thought you were married. You're too pretty to be unattached!" They finally met, and when they did, they instantly had something to talk about. She was surprised by how nervous he was. He didn't ask her on a date, so she sent him another note that read, "You are even more handsome up close. Please check the appropriate box: ☐ Yes, I would like to ask Alexandra on a date. ☐ No, I would not like to ask Alexandra on a date. Your answer must be mailed in before Wednesday or the offer will expire."

Dear Diary . . .
Sometimes you win, sometimes you lose. Tonight, I lost. While having dinner with Sandy, I was distracted by hit-and-miss eye contact with a handsome man. Feeling brave, I scrawled out a note—a tic-tac-toe game placing an X in the corner with the words, "Your move." The waiter made the delivery. Oh, no! An explosion of anger. Not anticipated. I immediately lost my line of vision with him as I slid down my chair. "Please don't make the connection," I said. Wrong!

Storming at me. "Oh, no!" Oh, yes! He was at my table,
yelling! Not American and a little bothered by my game.
Feeling like a piece of meat on a butcher's block, I got
chopped away. Once I was minced, he stormed away. Some-
times you win, sometimes you lose. One down for me.

———————

23

How to Be a
Secret Admirer

Everyone loves to receive notes of admiration; they're flattering. They are guaranteed to make a man's day. All you do is write a catchy little saying on small piece of paper. The best part about these notes is that you don't have to be outgoing to send them. Many shy women have found them to be great icebreakers.

When I was experimenting with material for this book, the note was the most well received technique I used on men. One night, for example, my business manager and I went to an upscale restaurant for a night of experimentation. We settled into our table comfortably as we arranged our observation notebooks, tape recorder, and pens. We were ready to go to work. We looked around the room and saw quite a few men out with other men. That was a good sign because we didn't want to cause any unnecessary arguments between couples with a playful experimental note. For two hours we anonymously sent 30 notes to unsuspecting men. Each man smiled when he first read the note. Most of the men sent the notes back through the waitresses, asking who "I" was so they could join me. One man received a note saying, "I'm writing a novel. Will you help? You look like the lead character. Story line . . . you start." We passed the note back and forth four times until he wrote, "I have an empty chair next to me. Why don't you join me and we can write together." To get more information about how the men felt, I interviewed them and asked them several questions about the experience. Every man I interviewed felt flattered that I had chosen him to send the note to. Each man was immediately curious and wanted to know who I was. None of the men had ever received a note. And all of them said they wanted to go out with me before they even met me. So, you see, a note is a powerful tool for meeting a man. The next time you are in a restaurant and see a man sitting alone, send him a note—it's a guaranteed date.

Originality is the key with a note. This does not mean you have to be creative; it simply means standing out from other women. Sure, you can write, "Hi. I'm Nancy, what's your name?" but that won't make him curious about you. To help you, I have listed quite a few lines I have "experimentally" tested and found to work very well.

There is only one no-no about sending a note. Avoid sexually related notes if you don't want the focus of your interaction to be about sex. First see whether you like him through the information you gather by passing notes.

Sample Lines to Use

Here are some examples of catchy notes to send to men. Feel free to make up your own.

- When I was in kindergarten I had a crush on a boy named Michael. You look just like him. Is your name Michael?
- You have a secret admirer. Try to guess who I am. Hint: I'm wearing black shoes.
- If you are interested in having a drink with me shout yes. Shout it loudly so I can hear you.
- I dreamt of a fairy-tale prince last night. Were you the one in it?
- I'm missing a shoe—have you seen it?

- They told me that I would meet a stranger in paradise. Would you like to identify yourself?
- I've been told I have a magnetic personality. I have just turned my power toward you. Is it working? Please respond.
- I'm trying to see your eye color, but you're so far away, would you care to move closer?
- What if I were a very good listener and you had something to say. Wouldn't it be great to have someone to share it with?
- Have you ever had the feeling that someone was watching you and thinking about you? Well, there is. It's me! What should I do?
- If you found yourself very attracted to someone sitting in the same restaurant, what would you do to break the ice?
- Would you care to help me pick some bananas?
- I enjoy looking into people's eyes. Could I try yours?
- I have a halo and I'm looking for someone to wear it. It might be your size.
- I'm having a little problem. You look like someone I would like to meet, but I don't have the nerve to say hello.
- This piece of paper is your invitation to join me at my table.
- You are the most handsome man in this room.
- When was the last time you received a note from a perfect stranger? Well, that's too long.
- I'm writing a novel. Will you help? You look like the leading character. Please respond through the waitress. Story line—you start.
- I'm writing a letter to my mother. What do you think I should write about our relationship? Please respond.
- I'm trying to solve a difficult relationship problem. Will you help? You name the problem.

What to Do When a Note Isn't Well Received

Very rarely, a note does not work. Take Maria, for example. She got creative and faxed a note to Bruce, a man she had just met at a party. She spent time talking with him, joking, and watched for signs of attraction. She was sure he was attracted to her, so she wrote the following note: "Hi, Bruce—My mailman informed me that my dinner invitation was lost in the mail. Please send another invite or call to confirm the details (555-5555). Sincerely, Maria Brown. . . . P.S. You have a certain charm about you. I'm curious!"

She faxed the note Monday morning and heard nothing. She called his office on Friday to verify that she had the right fax number. They told her she used the wrong number. In her excitement, she faxed the same note to the new number. She waited . . . and waited. Friday, Saturday, Sunday, Monday. . . . By Wednesday, she realized that he wasn't going to be responding and the invitation really wasn't lost. She felt embarrassed but lost nothing.

If you don't take a chance, you will never know how your note will be received. Keep in mind that Maria's unsuccessful experience was the first I have ever heard. For the times you feel unsure about sending notes to men, remember how well received they were from the men I interviewed in the restaurant.

Dear Diary . . .

My body shakes in his presence. Screaming with every glance. Alarms of attraction go off—emotional, physical, spiritual, sexual, cognitive. Beware! Danger ahead. Run before it's too late. No way. I feel an addiction coming on. With no consent, my body sins without his participation. It's incredible.

He approaches; suddenly cancerous dissatisfaction sets in. It's frozen in my grimace. Poor prognosis for approaching man. My body stiffens. It's too late now. "Hello" he says. Faking an unintelligible language, I mutter words that resemble "I'm pregnant, I'm looking for a husband." Looking away for a second to take a drink. Poof! He was gone. Recovering from my poor eyesight, I scan the crowd. My lucky day. I see another man . . . in the distance . . . oddly enough, my body shakes! Screaming with every glance . . . .

24

Graceful
Exit Lines

Do you know what to say to end a conversation with a man you've just met? In this chapter, you'll be reading about just that: the art of bringing an encounter to an end that will let him know whether you want to see him again. It's actually quite simple. If you come to the conclusion that the man does not qualify as someone you would like to date, you'll want to end the conversation with an exit line of rejection. If you want to explore the relationship further, you will end with an exit line of acceptance. Let's look at steps to exit gracefully when you have lost interest.

Basic Rules for Using Exit Lines

1. Avoid talking about personal topics. They energize a person's interest, which will fuel the conversation. Instead, talk about superficial topics.

2. Avoid using words that express emotions. Emotional words make a person think you want to continue talking. Instead, use thinking words. (See the examples.)

3. Have a sense of urgency, a reason to leave.

Example: Scene 1

I will be using an ongoing example in this chapter to demon-strate how exit lines work. Mary is at a formal singles party at a beautiful estate in Beverly Hills. She looks incredible and so does everyone else. Mary is on the prowl for a wealthy boyfriend, so she moves about with her radar on high. Feeling bold, she walks directly up to two men talking by the buffet table. During the introductions, she discovers one man is a limo driver and the other is a bodyguard. With this disclosure, she knows it is time to move on so she chats for a couple of minutes about how beau-tiful the house is (superficial talk). She doesn't want to waste her time, so she says, "It was nice meeting both of you. I need to find my friend (reason to leave); maybe we can talk again later."

When you meet someone you like, you naturally want to talk on an emotional level because it makes you feel closer to that person. Unfortunately, sometimes the desire to feel close is one-sided—his—and you feel annoyed by his imposing ques-tions that are too personal to share. There is only one good way to inform the man that you don't share his interest, and that is by using words that have nothing to do with feelings. See these examples:

Feeling Statements

1. I don't *feel* right tonight.
2. Do you *understand* what I mean?
3. I *hate* to *hurt* people's *feelings*.
4. I'm *sensitive* to material like that.
5. I don't *feel comfortable* doing that.

Thinking Statements

1. That problem can be *figured* out pretty easily.
2. Let me *think* about it for a while.
3. It *sounds understandable* to me.
4. That makes *sense* to me.
5. Can you *look* at it my way?

Example: Scene 2

A very good-looking man named Tom approaches Mary, and they begin a conversation. Tom's personality begins to surface, which warns Mary of his dependent nature: "I'm not dating her anymore, and it only lasted two months. We still live together but in separate rooms. She dates and I date. It used to *hurt* my feelings but doesn't anymore. I still *love* her, but it didn't work out." Tom is trying to solicit empathy from Mary by using feeling words, but it doesn't work because she has an aversion for dependent men. To bring the conversation to a close she uses thinking words that prevent the conversation from going any deeper: "It makes *sense* that she still lives there. It *sounds* like you have a sticky situation." She follows that line with another that has a sense of urgency to help her get away from him: "Oh, you know what? I was supposed to meet my friend by the door. She just hates to do things by herself. It was nice meeting you."

Feeling words and thinking words are how psychotherapists get their patients to disclose suppressed feelings and thoughts. The patient hour starts with small talk using thinking words and statements. Therapists begin to listen for the use of feeling words from the patient. In conversation, feeling words act like a key in a lock. When the therapist turns the key (uses the feeling word), the patient opens up, letting his wall down, and gets intimate with the therapist. This is why most patients feel closely bonded to a person they don't actually know. Near the end of a session, the therapist puts the key back in the lock and closes the emotions back up by using only thinking words and nonemotional topics. This is how conversations work with men, too. If you don't like them, don't reciprocate their emotional content. Instead, maintain unemotional small talk.

Exit Lines of Rejection: Examples

Here are several lines that should help you out of a conversation with "Mr. Wrong."

- I'm late for an appointment; I have to leave.
- Let me have your business card. I'll call you next week when I'm not so busy.
- Mention your "boyfriend/husband."
- I just got back together with my boyfriend.
- I have to be back at the office for a call.
- I have a meeting with my boss at 12:45.
- I live out of state; I'm going back tomorrow.
- I don't have time to date.
- I'm celibate.
- I'm meeting a friend; I don't want to be late.
- I'm parked in the red; I have to leave.
- I need to use the restroom.
- I have a phone call to make.
- I have to call home to say goodnight to my four children.

Exit Lines of Acceptance

Exit lines of acceptance are lines you use with a man you would like to see again. This means that you have qualified him through observation and conversation. You have arrived at the conclusion that he has advanced to candidacy and gets to have a second meeting with you.

Example: Scene 3

Mary resisted the dessert table until now. Oblivious to her surroundings, she goes to work picking up cheesecake, brownies, cookies, and pastries. With her plate overflowing, she sees someone heading for the last fudge bar. The other hand snatches it up and says, "I win. But if you'd like it, I'll let you have it. I've already eaten three." Looking up she sees the most beautiful eyes looking back at her. James introduces himself, and they indulge in conversation for three hours. Realizing the clock is about to strike midnight, she ends the conversation: "You are such an interesting man [personal compliment]. I've really enjoyed talking with you. I hope we can talk again soon" (clear message that she likes him). James walks her to her car, they exchange numbers, and he called her the minute he got home.

Tips to Exit

Men are hesitant to ask a woman out when they are unsure of how she feels. Many women unintentionally mislead men by talking to them when they aren't interested. This, of course, makes the man think you like him when you don't and makes both of you uncomfortable when he asks you on a date. Follow the tips here to communicate that you want to go on a date with him. In turn, he will ask you out.

1. Keep your mood upbeat and positive.
2. Don't drag out the initial encounter.
3. Pay him a personal compliment.
4. Get the message across that you are unequivocally interested in seeing him again.
5. Always be the one who ends the conversation. This makes the man want you more.

Example Exit Lines

Listed here are lines that men love to hear when they like you. If you think the feelings are mutual and you want to see him again, go ahead and try one of these:

- I've enjoyed talking with you. I'd like to do it again.
- I'm in a rush. But I'd like to talk with you when I have more time. You are very interesting.
- This may be forward, but I'd like to see you again.

There is only one way to get a man to ask you out, and that is to appear very interested in him. You need to make him feel special. Being forward leads to vulnerability, but the lack of initiative leads to a lonely life. Decide what you want—to take a risk or be alone.

Dear Diary . . .

Charlie will be at the sports bar for dinner tonight. My in-side spy, Laura, calls to inform me he's there. Tearing off my sweats, I slip into a dress. I'm off to "eat dinner." Applying lipstick, I steer my car down the road.

Panting with adrenaline, I enter the restaurant. I push my hair back, trying to look inconspicuous. A stranger? At least I am to him. Soon he'll know me, too.

Descending into the bar, I meander in Laura's direction. She passes, saying, "In the yellow shirt." I spot him. Noncha-lantly I pass his table. My peripheral vision takes note of his admiring attention. I ignore him and take looks from other men. Priming him. He's ready to meet me. I swing back in his direction.

Ready. Aim. Shoot . . . Devoured. Not to my palate's liking . . . I set him free. I head back home for a good night's rest.

25

In-Depth
Tracking Devices

You need to keep notes on potential partners: where you saw the man, the day, and the time. This will help you add some structure and purpose to your man search. Weekly, jot reminders in your calendar of places you saw the man or men. Don't waste your time jotting down every man who catches your fancy. Be selective. Remember to qualify the man first. The man should be attractive to you for two reasons. First, he should be your physical type. Second, he should be your emotional type. This means that if you are going to do a follow-up, then the man should pass your qualifying process.

Now what? Let's say the man is good for you. Now it's time to refer to the "follow-up sheet" described next. Place his name on your order form and go get him next week.

Example of a Follow-Up

Once every couple of weeks, Iris saw an attractive man at the local coffeehouse. He didn't appear to have a scheduled time he went there until she started keeping tabs on when she saw him. Suddenly she began to see a predictable pattern. He went there every other Wednesday at 9:20 A.M. Because of her new insight,

Iris began to schedule her calendar accordingly so that she would be there when he was. Eventually they began "noticing" each other, which led to talking. They have now been dating for six months and have coffee together every other Wednesday at 9:20 A.M.

How Girls Catch Boys in School

In high school, many boys and girls memorize each other's class schedules. Karen, for instance, knew that Tom would walk down the hall by the science room after third period. So, naturally, Karen would be there waiting for him to pass by. You see, high school teaches girls how to plot and scheme to get the boy they like. This was great then, and better now. Just think of how flattering it would be for the boy, now a man, to know that you went to so much trouble just because you thought he was special. He'd think it was wonderful!

Follow-Up Sheet

Use the following form to keep a running log of the men you run into in your daily contact with the world. When you see a man who catches your eye, simply fill in the blanks and try to run into him next week—same time, same place.

Man	Name	Day	Place	Time

Dear Diary . . .

    Woe is me! My heart reverberates with cutting pains of rejection. Histrionic? True. Take Ken, the source of my current heartache. We met four weeks ago. Chemistry was observed as the kindling fire grew between us. He was captivated by me describing myself as an intelligent, playful beauty. He swept me off my feet with a dinner invitation to Hawaii and a second date to Canada. A little misunderstanding turned into a lot of anger and doomsday for the budding romance.

    The final breath of our union took place today. He punished me with no phone call. Instead, I should have assumed my deserving position high on my pedestal, being bestowed with deserving gifts in appreciation for today's holiday— my birthday. Unforgivable!

26

Handling Rejection

Sean Connery was voted the best-looking man one year by *People* magazine. Is he your type? Many women would not give him the time of day. Do you think of that as rejecting Mr. Connery? Of course not. Then why is it any different for you when a man doesn't respond to your flirtatious glances? People tend to overpersonalize another's lack of interest, interpreting it as rejection.

It is definitely uncomfortable when a man doesn't return your interest in him. There seems to a silent rule that says, "You must like me when I like you." It is easy to become upset by the perceived rejection, but it doesn't always make logical sense. Rejection usually results in a woman feeling angry, confused, and embarrassed. These are normal reactions and should be expected. What isn't normal is a common reaction many women have. They irrationally believe that the man isn't interested in them because of some imperfection or fatal flaw. This type of thinking leads to feelings of sorrow, depression, and hopelessness rather than the more short-lived feelings. These are the women who suffer with their self-esteem and feel overwhelmed by a rejection, viewing it as something being wrong with themselves.

Think back to a time when you felt rejected by a man. Which feelings did you feel? Do you remember the thoughts you had? Were your thoughts rational or irrational? Did they hold any trueness or not?

Ashley stopped at a restaurant on her way home from work. She sat at the bar while she waited for the takeout. While sitting there, she struck up a conversation with Phillip, who seemed to be engrossed in what they talked about. Phillip encouraged her to stay and have dinner with him because he enjoyed the company so much, so she stayed. He walked her out to her car, and they exchanged cards when he said that he wanted to see her again. She drove away filled with excitement with thoughts of his handsome face. A week went by, and he hadn't called so she called his office just to hear his secretary say, "He isn't in. Would you like to leave a message?" After leaving a few messages over a period of a week, she gave up and felt terrible.

Does Ashley have a real reason to feel terrible? Certainly not. Disappointment would have been more appropriate. What did she really know about Phillip besides that he enjoyed the conversation? Her experience isn't being rejected, though. He could have had a good reason that he didn't call her. Maybe he got back together with his ex. Perhaps he got test results back that said he was positive for some kind of disease. What I am trying to get across here is that women shouldn't attribute personal defects with why a man isn't interested in her.

Another illustration of rejection comes from Eileen. She met Jim at a singles party, and a magic chemistry developed between the two of them. As a matter of fact, they ended up making out in the parking lot for an hour before they said goodbye. He said he would call, and he never did. Later Eileen found out that Jim had a wife. He didn't reject her—he used her because he found her attractive.

When a woman feels rejected, it is usually because she feels that she is being abandoned by the man. To explain the abandonment, she comes up with irrational reasons for why she drove him away. This type of thinking is self-focused rather than other-focused. By using *self-focused,* I am describing a woman who reacts with childish or narcissistic emotional immaturity. She is like a hurt child. This is not bad; it just hurts when it happens to you. The best way to deal with it is to allow your development to mature into an adult reaction that is reality based, rational, and other-focused. I've listed a few examples of these types of thinking to help you understand a little more clearly:

Self-Focused

What's wrong with me?

Maybe he doesn't think I'm pretty enough.

I must have bored him.

I wonder what I did wrong that turned him off.

Other-Focused

Something must be going on in his life.

He's probably involved with someone else.

He might be commitment phobic.

He was a great guy. It's too bad it can't work out.

Every man and every woman have different physical and emotional types that they are attracted to. Just because you may find a man desirable does not mean that you are his type as well. Does this mean that you are being rejected if he turns you down for a date? Think about it. What are you really losing? Certainly it shouldn't shake your self-esteem. He doesn't even know you. When you feel that you are being rejected, think of reasons, other than yourself, that he may not be responding favorably to you.

Reasons That a Man Might Reject You

1. He may be in a relationship already.
2. He might be gay.
3. He may be grieving the loss of someone close.
4. You may remind him of a woman he dislikes.
5. He may be worried about his job.
6. He may be worried about some aspects of his health.
7. He may be late for an important engagement.

The reasons are endless. None of these items have the slightest connection to you. So don't take them personally.

As for another case, read on to see what happened to Veronica. She was captivated with Mike, whom she worked with on a volunteer basis helping needy children. Their friendly conversations lasted for six months, and she couldn't understand why Mike wouldn't ask her out. She knew he was attracted to her too. One day she asked another volunteer whether Mike had a girlfriend. The woman laughed at her and said, "Of course not—don't you know he's a priest?" It was unbelievable to her but made a lot of sense.

Accepting Yourself:
Seven Rules to Live By

If you are the kind of woman who blames yourself for a man not liking you, read the following list of ways to help you learn to like yourself more. With practice, you will begin to love yourself more and value who you are, even if someone else doesn't.

1. *Accept yourself.* As a human being, you are, by definition, imperfect. Come to terms with the fact that you are a worthwhile woman, despite your inadequacies or mistakes.

2. *Respect yourself.* Recognize your abilities and talents. Acknowledge your competence and achievements, and take pride in them.

3. *Trust yourself.* Learn to listen to the voice within you and let your intuition be your guide. No one knows you better than you do. Rely on your sense of self.

4. *Love yourself.* Be happy to spend time by yourself. Learn to appreciate your company, and be glad you're you.

5. *Stretch yourself.* Be willing to change and grow, to take risks and dare to be vulnerable.

6. *Look at challenges as opportunities for growth.*

7. *Imagine the year 2000.* Where do you want to be, and whom do you want to be?

Taking care of yourself is the foundation for high self-esteem. If you feel good about yourself, then others will feel good about you too.

Developing Self-Confidence: Where Does Self-Confidence Come From?

People are born with self-confidence. As you grow up, all the good and bad things that happen to you affect your self-image. The only way to build confidence is to believe in yourself.

Even if you had a deficit growing up and currently have a lack in self-confidence, you can build it up on your own, by practicing to have self-esteem. This means that you can act the way self-confident people act, move the way they move, say the things they say, and, most important, practice the positive self-statements they use.

People who appear to "have it all" don't automatically have a lot of self-confidence. Appearances can be deceptive. Some women feel confident in most areas of their lives but lack confidence in relating to men. Rita, for instance, knew that people liked her, she made friends easily, but it was a different story when it came to her perspective of men. When she saw a man she was attracted to, she would say, "I'm sure he won't like me." Her friend Linda, on the other hand, had a great deal of confidence and expected men to like her when they met her. A woman's level of confidence has its roots in what her thoughts are. People perceive her thoughts and will treat her accordingly.

The following steps will help you build your confidence, not only in your everyday life but with men also. The more you tell yourself the following statements, the sooner they will become your own thoughts and beliefs about who you are.

1. Like yourself as you are. Don't think you have to change to get a man to like you.
2. Believe in yourself. You have a lot to offer a relationship as you are.

3. Trust yourself to do the right thing.
4. Respect yourself for who you are.
5. Forgive past hurts. Don't let past relationships prevent you from getting involved in new relationships.
6. Say, "I can" rather than "I can't."
7. Don't rely on others to make you feel worthwhile.
8. Believe that you deserve to be treated with respect.

In a magazine survey (*Men's Health,* December 1995), the editors asked men, "What makes her so sexy?" This is what the men said: Personality (62 percent), beauty (55 percent), sense of humor (48 percent), smile (47 percent), intelligence (47 percent), legs (45 percent), shapeliness (44 percent), breasts (43 percent), eyes (43 percent), buttocks (42 percent), hair (37 percent), voice (34 percent), and height (16 percent).

Being sexy is a characteristic that confident women send out because they feel good about themselves. If you don't feel good about yourself, then use these characteristics to judge objectively who you are. If you have a cynical personality, then it will negatively affect a significant portion of a man's impression of you. If you have a great smile, what an easy way to add points! Make the most of what you have by viewing it positively rather than negatively.

It Begins in Childhood

Many women are interested in the psychological aspects of why they turned out the way they did. This section describes seven types of parents a woman may have, with the characteristics that grow out of each type. All of these styles can cause women to feel inadequate.

1. *Overly critical parent.*—As an adult, the woman is a perfectionist, critical with herself, and feels that she is never good enough.
2. *Lack of parent through childhood loss.*—As an adult, the woman feels abandoned in relationships, has a void that can't

be filled, may develop overdependencies on others, and may be prone to addictions to fill the "void."

3. *Abusive parent.*—As an adult, the woman feels insecure, has difficulty trusting others, has a tendency to get in abusive relationships, and has difficulty with intimate relationships.

4. *Alcoholic or drug-abusing parent.*—As an adult, the woman tends to get involved with alcoholic men and has a poor sense of personal identity.

5. *Negligent parent.*—As an adult, the woman tends to feel worthless, has a sense of loneliness, and tends to neglect her own needs or discount them.

6. *Overprotective parent.*—As an adult, the woman has a difficult time trusting others, is afraid to take risks, gets involved in dependent relationships, and settles for men who are not her equal.

7. *Rejecting parent.*—As an adult, the woman feels that she is not wanted, doubts her own abilities, and tends to reject herself.

Do any of these categories remind you of yourself? The point in remembering the past is not to blame your parents but to realize where your lack of self-esteem came from. Your parents did the best they knew how to do. It is time to build your self-esteem up by reparenting yourself. You can do this by doing three things. One, meet your basic needs. Two, make time to nurture yourself. Three, discover what you can provide for yourself and what you can get from a man. Many books take you step-by-step through the reparenting process, so read them if you need the help.

———

Dear Diary . . .
   Watching him . . . watching her. My thoughts stop visually at a poison shop. Grass killer for the weed in my garden. His titillated mind becomes consumed. He approaches her to get a closer look. He sees beauty where I see ugliness.

He visualizes his gloved hands firmly gripping the body of this new strain, pulling it close to his eyes in a scrutiny of lust. "Poison." His mind becomes consumed by the floating seedings of temptation.

His thoughts turn real, and in my absence he waters her generously. I pull her from the ground hoping she'll die. With an ultimatum, he assures me she's gone. As the weeks go by, his restless memories of affection create a craving he can't resist.

The spark of their reunion ignites our garden like a blazing brushfire destroying all but the gate that was once kept closed to protect us from threats. I fall to the ground in my pain, watching the glory of their new garden blossom on the horizon.

———————

27

Dating the Second (or Third, or Fourth . . .) Time Around

If you have you just finished a long-term relationship and are nervous about dating, then this is the chapter for you. Although the last relationship had problems, at least it offered the comfort of knowing what to expect from your partner. Most women fret over the typical first date: "Is he going to call?" "What am I supposed to wear?" "Where should we go?" "What am I supposed to talk about?" "What should I order at the restaurant?" "What am I supposed to drink?" In this chapter, each of these issues will be addressed individually so you have nothing to worry about.

Before you begin, fill in these blanks:

1. My biggest fear about dating is_____
2. I tend to avoid dating because_____
3. My resource person for fashion is_____
4. My resource person for food is_____
5. My resource for drinks is_____
6. My resource person for relationship advice is_____

If you find that you don't have a network of resource people to help support you, then it's time to find them. These people can be girlfriends, authors, or anyone. Just make sure you have access to them when you need them. Dating can be unnecessarily nerve-racking, so the more support and guidance you have, the easier it will be.

When Is He Going to Call?

One of the most stressful parts about dating is waiting to see whether a man is actually going follow his statement "I'll call you" with a call. A lot of men use that line because they don't know how to say they aren't interested in you.

For the man who is going to call, there are unwritten guidelines they follow that tell them when to call. When a man meets a woman he likes, the first thing he wants to do is call her, but he stops himself. He knows that if he calls too soon or too often, he will appear overly anxious. If he waits too long, then the woman will be annoyed and won't be eager to go out with you. By far the most accurate rule they follow is the "two-day" rule. When a man wants to make the best impression on a woman, he will wait 48 hours before he calls her. It doesn't matter how well they got along when they met; he knows that if he calls too soon, she won't be as anxious to talk with him, so he grits his teeth and waits 48 hours.

Charted here are the guidelines for you to follow to let you know when a man you like will call you. The first column marks the day you met him. The second column is the day he will call you. The third column is the day he will ask you out based on the day he met you. Take, for instance, Janet. She and Barry met on Monday. That means that he will wait two days to call her, which puts his call on Wednesday night, and he will ask her out for the upcoming weekend.

WHEN HE IS LIKELY TO CALL

Day you met	Day he will call	Day he will ask you out for
Monday	Wednesday	Upcoming weekend
Tuesday	Thursday	If he detects that you already have plans, he will say he's busy that weekend too, but would like to get together the next weekend.
Wednesday	Friday afternoon	He will leave a message because he can't call you on Friday night, saying that he will call you early next week about getting together.
Thursday	Sunday afternoon	Upcoming weekend
Friday	Sunday afternoon	Upcoming weekend
Saturday	Monday evening	Upcoming weekend or lunch during the week
Sunday	Tuesday	Upcoming weekend or lunch during the week

The exceptions to the two-day rule are Wednesday and Thursday. If he calls you two days after meeting you on one of those days, it places his call on a "date night." He doesn't want to feel like he has to ask the woman out that night. Remember, he may already have plans but just wants to talk to you. On the other hand, he doesn't want to appear too eager by asking you out so soon. However, if he does ask you out for that night, turn him down or you will appear too easy. Be very friendly, but tell him you had already made plans with your best friend but you can see him next weekend.

Men most often call on Sunday afternoon or evening because it is the least threatening night to call. There are some men who ignore these rules because they don't have the self-control to wait so long, and they have the confidence to know it's all right to chase you.

What Not to Wear on a Date

The moratorium is over and you've decided that it is time to start dating again. It sounds great until you begin to ponder the nuances of getting dressed for a date. Let's talk for a moment about clothes. Do you know what to wear on a date? Here are the common mistakes that women make with their clothes on a first date:

- Wearing wrinkled clothes
- Underdressing (wearing sweats or jeans)
- Not dressing for the occasion
- Not shaving legs or underarms
- Not showering before the date
- Wearing too much perfume
- Wearing noticeable hair gel
- Wearing clothes that don't fit right
- Wearing the wrong colors
- Wearing old clothes
- Having holes in clothes
- Wearing old shoes
- Wearing dirty or stained clothes
- Wearing too much jewelry
- Wearing large prints
- Not wearing earrings
- Wearing business clothes on a weekend date
- Having noticeable panty lines
- Wrapping shirts around the waist
- Wearing huge shoulder pads
- Wearing clothes that cut into your fat
- Not wearing fresh makeup

What Do Men Like Women to Wear on a Date?

The rules for dressing for a date are simple. First, avoid all of the dating mistakes mentioned earlier. Next, if the date is a casual event, wear casual clothing such as a summer dress, shorts, or casual pants and a sweater. For dinner, wear a simple dress that shows off your figure. This does not mean you have to have a perfect figure; it means accentuating your best parts. For instance, if you have nice legs, show your legs; if you have nice shoulders, bare them. A great book to consult for dressing is *Dress for Success,* which can be found in any bookstore.

Overall, men like women to be feminine and ladylike. Although an old pair of jeans is comfortable, save them for when you are alone. With men, follow these guidelines to be safe:

1. Men like women to dress appropriately for the occasion.
2. Men prefer dresses to pants. The most preferred is the long dress.
3. Men love hair on a woman. It can be any length, as long as it is feminine. They prefer it worn down in the daytime and up for the evening.
4. Men like little to medium amounts of makeup on a woman.
5. Men prefer a feminine style of dressing. They don't like oversized clothing which conceal your contours.
6. Men don't like clothing that is too revealing. A little skin showing is more attractive than a lot of skin.
7. Men don't like women to dress like a man (suits, pants).
8. Men prefer heels to flat shoes.
9. A man's preferred jewelry items on a woman is a small to medium pair of earrings; second choice is a necklace, especially pearls.
10. Men prefer almost any other clothing to a pair of jeans—this is especially true of men in the upper class.

Let's take the example of Denise to illustrate exactly how important clothing can be on a date. Denise is a thin, plain-looking, 41-year-old woman who liked to hide her figure behind oversized clothing. She wore her hair in an unflattering short haircut. Although her clothes were very expensive, she still projected an unattractive look. When she met Lee, it was on a Friday casual day at work. Lee assumed her frumpiness was due to the day since everyone was underdressed. When Lee picked Denise up for the date, he was disappointed because she looked as bad as the day he met her. Her hair was still unstyled, she had no makeup on, she had bulky shoulder pads under her nonrevealing bulky sweater, pants, and flat shoes. If Denise had been smart and wanted to keep Lee's interest, she would have dressed more like Lee's previous girlfriend, who loved being a woman and it showed. She wore figure-conscious clothing, dresses, had feminine mannerisms, and wore her hair seductively the way he loved it. He knew he had made a mistake with Denise and never called her again.

Restaurant Ordering: Food

The main complaint women have about a dinner date is the pressure they feel when it comes to ordering an entree. They want to make a good impression on the man by what they order. Many women would rather not go to dinner than to be confronted with this anxiety. I consulted with managers of top restaurants for tips to help take some of the fear away. If you follow their advice, you will have no problems appearing competent in what and how you order.

The restaurant managers have given me a list of food found in most restaurants. This list should relieve your anxiety about what to order because you will already know what you will be eating before you get there.

Salads

Most dinner dates start off with an appetizer or salad before the dinner arrives. Although a woman may be hungry, her nervousness causes her to decline this portion of the meal. Women, more often than men, are concerned not only with what they order but how they appear eating the food. This is why a salad is a good item to order. Most restaurants prepare salads with bite-size leaves, but don't hesitate to use your knife to cut the larger leaves of lettuce. Don't take the chance of folding the lettuce with your fork—you may be asking for trouble. When cutting lettuce, cut each bit separately rather than making a mess of your salad by cutting it all at once. Two basic kinds of salads are available in almost every restaurant: Caesar salads and garden salads.

Appetizers and Main Entrees

An appetizer is an alternative to the salad and is a starter food like the salad, eaten before the main course. It is difficult to find one kind of appetizer for each kind of restaurant because menu items are usually based on the type of restaurant you are in. For instance, on a Chinese menu you will find items like spring rolls and dumplings. On an Italian menu, a typical appetizer is calamari. But don't worry: there is still an easy way to get through the night stress-free. Depending on how uncomfortable you are, you can pick and choose from the suggestions listed here. What's guaranteed is that you will be able to come across to your date as though you know what you like and have confidence in knowing these things.

1. Decide which restaurant you will be going to in advance.
2. Call the restaurant at an off-peak hour and ask for help making menu choices.
3. Go to the restaurant before the date and read the menu, or pick up a paper menu to take home with you.

Hostesses of most restaurants are extremely helpful during off-peak hours. All you have to do is call the restaurant during a quiet hour (10–11 A.M. and 2:30–3:30 P.M.) and tell the hostess that you would like to ask her a few questions. Make a list of concerns before calling. You may ask, "What is an easy food item to eat?" or "What kind of appetizer and main dish go well together?" Most hostesses will be glad to help you. Be honest and let her know that you will be there on a date and don't want to make a fool out of yourself. She'll give you her expert advice on ordering, and you'll have one less thing to worry about.

When ordering entrees, you will have to follow the previous guidelines because all restaurants offer such different foods.

Restaurant Ordering: Drinks

Not everyone drinks alcohol, so I've divided the drink section into nonalcoholic and alcoholic drinks. Again, the managers at various restaurants have devised a no-fail approach to ordering drinks while on a date. All of the drinks listed here are in all restaurants. These tips will help to relieve needless anxiety on a date when your mind goes blank. That way you will be able to focus more on what is important: qualifying your date.

Nonalcoholic Drinks

Predinner Drinks

Pelegrino—sparkling water served with or without a lemon twist

Traditional—soda, water, iced tea

Dinner Drinks

All of the preceding drinks

Nonalcoholic beer

After-Dinner Drinks

Coffee

Espresso—a strong coffee, served in a tiny coffee cup. The preferred way to drink it is with real sugar as opposed to a sweetener. It is served with a tiny lemon rind. You take the lemon rind, hold it over the cup, twist, and rub the rind around the rim of the cup.

Cappuccino—steamed milk and coffee; mocha varieties include chocolate flavor. It is served in a coffee cup with whipped cream on top.

Alcoholic Drinks

How often have you drawn a blank when it comes time to order a drink? There seem to be so many choices to choose from. Should you be conservative and order wine or have a mixed drink? Ordering alcohol can be an overwhelming decision while on a date. That is why I have created this drink list with the help of an expert bartender, a single mother, who has watched many women over the years go through this uncomfortable process while on dates.

Predinner Drinks

   Wine—see below

   Margarita—sweet margarita mix and tequila

   Bloody Mary—tomato juice mix and vodka

   Screwdriver—orange juice and vodka

   Sea Breeze—Vodka, cranberry juice, and grapefruit juice

Dinner Drinks

   Red dinner wines—cabernet (ka-bair-nay), Merlot (mair-lo)

   White wines—chardonnay (shar-den-ay), sauvignon blanc (so-ven-yawn blahnc)

   All predinner drinks

After-Dinner Drinks

   Grand Marnier—orange-flavored liqueur

   Bailey's and coffee—sweet Irish cream with coffee

   Kahlua and coffee—sweet coffee-flavored liqueur with coffee

   Dessert wines

As you know, this kind of insecurity only lasts for a few dates. By that time women typically feel comfortable enough with the man that they are able to read a menu or think clearly again. These guidelines are especially good for the woman who feels unsure about herself early on in a dating relationship. However, any woman can build her confidence by having a ready-made decision in the case that she freezes up.

Dear Diary . . .

I met him at a piano bar. Mike. He caressed my heart when he looked at me. It was stolen the moment he said hello. Perfection. Not in a literal sense. Just in my eyes . . . my adoring eyes.

His warmth glued my heart together. He made me feel wanted, safe. Vulnerability seeped out when he was around. I pretend to be strong.

Never a kiss. Only a touch. Never an action. Only a thought.

Words of like. Thoughts of love. My love. His love. Our love.

28

Summarizing the Search Formula

In this book, you have learned many new things to help find a desirable man. It can be easy to forget things, so I have summarized the highlights of the flirting formula. The six main steps are as follows:

1. Scan the environment.
2. Take your place.
3. Deal with nervousness.
4. Verbal encounter.
5. Qualifying the man.
6. Use your exit lines.

The Goal of the Formula

Many women feel uncomfortable when they see a man they would like to meet. Consequently, their focus switches from how they can meet the man to feelings of inexperience and self-consciousness. Because of this, I have created a road map for women to follow. It will take the uncertainty out of your search and replace it with predictable guidelines to follow each time.

Step 1: Scan the Environment

Take note of what's going on around you. Wherever you are,
walk around the entire place to find the man who meets your
requirements. When you see the man, pay attention. Is he
alone? Is he with friends? Is he with a woman? If so, could she
possibly be a friend or associate? How much time do you have
to flirt with him?

An Example of Step 1

Picture yourself in the public library. It's your lunch hour, and
you've decided to take the time to scan not only the books but
also the patrons for a potential partner. You have roughly 30
minutes. Now walk into the library and walk around to create
a mental map of the floor plan. That way you know where the
men are and where to position yourself. Of course, you want
to put yourself next to a man whom you're attracted to. Keep
in mind what your physical and emotional type of man is and
stick to it. Now move to step 2.

Step 2: Take Your Place

All right, you've walked around and discovered who's in the
place. Now it's time to position yourself. Keep in mind three
things at this time:

1. Proximity
2. Body language
3. Get him to notice you before the two of you meet.

Proximity

You're in the library again. You need to sit within six feet of
him. That's talking range. Anything further than that makes it
too uncomfortable to have a conversation.

Body Language

Position yourself facing the man, turning your body toward him. That gives him the message that you're attracted to him. He may not be aware of this, but his subconscious is and he will respond accordingly. See Chapter 20 on nonverbal communication for more details.

Men Take Awhile to Judge

Now it's time to get him to notice you. One of the interesting things about women is the fact that it takes them three seconds to tell whether they're attracted to a man. It takes men thirty seconds to know. So it's important to give him a few seconds to watch you. That way you can see whether he likes you and determine whether he's attracted to you. By the time you sit down next to him or walk past him, he already knows whether he likes you or not. The body language that you read will accurately reflect his feelings.

Step 3: Dealing with Nervousness

Being nervous is a natural part of flirting because it makes a woman feel at the mercy of a man's judgment. Although being nervous may seem like a bad thing, there are some positives:

1. Regardless of how nervous you are, people are not able to tell.
2. As you talk, the nervousness goes away.
3. Men expect you to be nervous around them.

Read Chapter 18, "How to Master Nervousness," for details.

Step 4: Verbal Encounters

It's time to use your entrance lines or entrance actions to actually initiate a conversation. The whole point of an entrance line is to convey a message to the man that you would like to meet him. You want to talk to him. You're curious about him. You're attracted to him. It's very flattering to him. So, it really doesn't matter what you say or what you do. He's going to know the real reason that you're using a line or an action, anyway. It means that you're interested in him, and he knows that.

The No-Fail Approach

It's a good idea to stay focused on one very successful entrance line: the question. I referred to it earlier a couple of times. In summary, first say "Excuse me." Next, you ask the man an open-ended question. Lastly, you respond with a follow-up statement that is personal in nature. See Chapter 21 for more details.

An Example of an Open-Ended Question

Woman: Excuse me. (step 1)

Man: Yes?

Woman: I've noticed that you come to the library often. What do you enjoy reading? (step 2)

Man: I love biographies about successful people.

Woman: How interesting. I also enjoy stories of high achievement. Do you have a favorite? (step 3)

Man: The one about Donald Trump was very interesting.

Why Use Open-Ended Questions?

Don't sell yourself short by using closed-end questions. Instead, open-ended questions are a must for the following reasons:

1. They lead to more than just a yes or no response.
2. They naturally lead into a conversation.
3. They allow people to respond on their own terms.
4. They allow you to get a lot of information about the man up front.
5. By being the who asks the questions, it puts you in control.

Entrance Actions

An alternative to an entrance line is an entrance action—using a behavior rather than using words to start an encounter with a desirable man.

A Note for the Man

By far, the most successful approach is the note. This is exactly what it sounds like. You send a note to him—a secret admirer note. It can be done secretly, in which you conceal your identity. Or, you reveal your identity. Refer to Chapter 23, "How to Be a Secret Admirer," for more details.

Examples of Other Entrance Actions

1. Invite yourself to sit at his table.
2. Stand next to him.
3. Send him a drink.
4. Touch his arm.
5. Smile at him.
6. Ask him to do a favor for you.

Step 5: How to Disqualify the Man

When you meet a man, you want to know as much about him as you possibly can. I call this disqualifying a man. It's the time you use to see whether he measures up to what you are looking for in a happy relationship. There are two ways to disqualify a man: through observation and through conversation.

Observe What's Going On

When you observe a man, watch his behaviors for signs of the problems that got you into bad relationships in the past. For instance, you dated a man who smoked and refuse to follow that path again, but every man you meet seems to smoke. When you are out, you need to slow your pace down and

observe the men you like from afar. Do you see him smoking?
If he is smoking, he's been disqualified. If not, you can move
on to the next step—qualifying him through conversation.

Conversation Is So Telling

A conversation should have one primary goal: to see whether
the man meets your qualifications for a healthy relationship.
During the conversation, use your time wisely by lightly touching on areas that have led to the ending of previous relationships. See Chapter 16 for more details.

Step 6: Exit Lines of Acceptance

Exit lines are the final words you use in a conversation with a
man. There are two types of exit lines:

1. Exit lines of rejection
2. Exit lines of acceptance

Exit Lines of Rejection

Exit lines of rejection are lines you use when you decide that a
man does not qualify. This means that you don't want to talk to
him further for whatever reason. The lines are gently delivered
to the man, yet effective. The first thing you do is have the conversation return to a level using thinking words only and no
feeling words. Be sure to stick to nonpersonal conversation.
More important, exit lines need to have a sense of urgency that
gives you a reason to leave. See Chapter 24 for examples of actual exit lines to use.

Exit Lines of Acceptance

If you like a man and want him to ask you out on a date, then
you need to convey that message. By using an exit line, it lets
him know unequivocally that you are interested in him. Many
women get so caught up in playing games that they don't let

the man know they are interested in him. Then you wonder why the man did not show interest in you. Well, if a man has even the slightest hint that you will reject him, then he is not likely to go out with you. So, let your guard down a little and convey your interest. That does not mean you are being too easy, just that you like him. See Chapter 24 for more details.

29

Happily
Ever After

In this book, you have learned a lot of techniques and ideas. According to motivational speaker Tom Hopkins, a person must be exposed to new material six times before she is able to retain 62 percent of what she has learned. By reading this book once, your retention rate will be very low. Because of this, I advise you to review your weak areas at least six times. Like anything new, it takes a lot of practice to be comfortable using it. What I am saying is that you will feel some level of discomfort applying what you have learned. Your motivation for continuing is knowing that you will have to change your old patterns to find a desirable man.

Turning "It" Off and On

Marilyn Monroe was a beautiful, alluring woman. She was described as being able to turn "it" on and off. During the times when "it" was turned off, she was able to walk anonymously down a crowded street regardless of her physical beauty. However, when she turned "it" on, people were drawn to her inner radiations of charisma. No one ever officially defined what "it" was, so I suppose we will never know.

An Equally Powerful Concept

An equally strong idea for you to consider is the techniques in this book. These techniques will give you the knowledge base and skills to be able to do what Marilyn Monroe did: have people drawn to you. You will be able to use your skills, your "it," to draw men to you.

Be like Marilyn Monroe and turn your "it" on during your scheduled search days. On your days off, you can turn "it" off and go back to being unnoticed. Just keep in mind the power you possess over men's reactions to you by having with you your new ability to turn "it" on and turn "it" off.

Because you are reading this book, I assume that you have experienced a failed relationship. Kareem Abdul Jabbar recently spoke at a success seminar. He knows how persevering through the failures can help you attain success. "Don't get on your case when you don't do well. You won't learn how to win until you know how to lose," Kareem advises those who feel like giving up too soon. In dating, it is very easy to give up, but if you are persistent and go after what you want, you will succeed in finding the relationship to make you happy. Remember, you have already learned how to fail; with the help of this book, you now know how to win. I wish you a lot of luck in your search for a great man.

Index

actual

Molestation, *see* Sexual abuse
Monroe, Marilyn, 206–207
Movies, 85–86
Mr. Right
  characteristics, 50–54
  finding, 30–37
Musicians
  characteristics, 71
  dressing for, 75

N

Needs, basic, 12–18
Negativity, overcoming, 138–140
Nervousness
  attractive aspects, 134–135
  body language and, 9
  getting over, 133–134
  managing, 137
  mastering, 133–140
    techniques for, 135–137
  signs of, 133–134
Newspapers
  dates and, 82–89
  finding men through, 79–81
Noncommitting men, 48–50
Note, *see* Secret admirer note
Nourishment, 13

O

Observation, *see also* Eyes
  gazing
    evaluating, 130–132
    interpreting, 127–132
    types, 121–124
  process, 118–120

The office visit, 164
Open-ended questions, 154–155
Organizations, 78–79
Other-focused type, 182–183
Outdoor activities, 86

P

Parents, dysfunctional, 186–187
Parks, 101–102
Partners, *see* Relationships
Passive approach, 112
People magazine survey, 181
Personality types, *see also* Characteristics
  other-focused, 183
  professions and, 59–60,
    67–72
  self-focused, 182–183
Phone calls, 190–192
Physical attraction
  evaluating, 24–27
  needs and, 18–20
Physical disabilities, 8
Platonic relationships,
  147–152
Police officers
  characteristics, 69–70
  dressing for, 75
Professions
  personality types in, 59–60
    analyzing, 66–72
  selection, birth order and,
    61–66
Professors
  characteristics, 68–69
  dressing for, 75